SYDENHAM
AND FOREST HILL

history & guide

SYDENHAM
AND FOREST HILL

history & guide

Joan P. Alcock

The History Press

frontispiece View looking over the Crystal Palace terraces towards Sydenham, 2004.

First published in 2005 by Tempus Publishing Ltd

Reprinted in 2011 by
The History Press
The Mill, Brimscombe Port
Stroud, Gloucestershire GL5 2QG
www.thehistorypress.co.uk

British Library Cataloguing in Publication Data.
A catalogue record for this book is available from the British Library.

ISBN 978 0 7524 3406 3

Typesetting and origination by Tempus Publishing.
Printed in Great Britain

Contents

Preface and acknowledgements

With 'the advent of the Croydon railway in 1836' Sydenham 'sprang into prominence as a London suburb. This event, in conjunction with the erection of the Crystal Palace on the summit of the hill eighteen years later, practically converted the erstwhile hamlet into the well-populated residential district of today', wrote C. Edgar Thomas in *The Antiquary* in October 1913, although he opined gloomily that Sydenham could not 'compete with the majority of other London suburbs in the matter of historical associations and antiquarian lore'.

Ninety years later, the 'well-populated district' described by Thomas has undergone further changes. The bombing in the Second World War altered the pattern of housing; the growth of suburbia has resulted in the building of houses not only on wasteland but also on garden plots. The number of people, their multiethnic cultures and the variety of shops in the area might startle him. The Crystal Palace was lost in 1936 and the admired park has become a sad reminder of what once was the pride of the district. Yet a modern Thomas can walk in that park and the other parks in the area and recognise their value to the community.

Sydenham and Forest Hill have never been independent communities; they have always been overshadowed by their attachment to Lewisham. Yet they still have a distinct character. This history focuses on the growth and development of Sydenham and Forest Hill from open common land in Kent to the sprawling suburb of Greater London that it is today. More detailed accounts of individual subjects are found in various monographs. Individual houses and events are described in John Coulter's excellent histories and the Lewisham Local History Society Journals have articles relating to the history of Sydenham and Forest Hill.

Every person who writes a local history is indebted to those persons who have corrected and improved the manuscript and helped the research in a variety of ways. I am particularly indebted to John Coulter, who read the text and saved me from a number of errors. Stephen Grindley of the Sydenham Society was generous with his time in reading and correcting several drafts and arranging for a loan of photographs. Pat Trembath, chairman of the Sydenham Society, gave details about developments at Bell Green, and Gordon Dennington gave help with the chapter on the Second World War. Melvyn Harrison, chairman of the Crystal Palace Foundation, provided help with the Crystal Palace chapter. The late Margaret Roxan, Fellow of the Institute of Classical Studies, allowed me to use her translation of, and provided information on, the Roman *diplomata*. J.D. Hill, curator of the Iron Age collections at the British Museum, provided details of the bronze serpent found on Westwood Common. Christopher Sparey-Green allowed me to use information on prehistoric finds. Professor Bryan Reuben, London South Bank University, made valuable suggestions for the improvement of the text. Robert Wegrzyrn, London South Bank University, was a great help in the production of maps and photographs. Phyllis Kern yet again helped with meticulous checking of the manuscript, photographs and proofs.

Others who have helped in my research include Jan Piggott, Keeper of Archives and Rare Books at Dulwich College, David Allen, Librarian of the Horniman Museum, Graham Bickley, Damian Falkowski, and Peter Walker of the Dietrich Bonhoeffer church.

The following individuals and organisations to which copyright belongs have kindly given permission for illustrations to be reproduced: Audrey Hammond for the colour illustration of 'The White Swan and the Crystal Palace Parade'; Damian Falkowski for the colour illustration of Ash Tree Cottage; Joan Read for the photograph of the head of Paxton on page 69; the Dietrich Bonhoeffer church for the photograph on page 47 and the colour illustration of the Dietrich Bonhoeffer church windows; Stephen Grindley and the Sydenham Society for the photographs on pages 21, 27, 29, 39, 40, 43, 45 (large photograph), 46 (upper photograph), 48, 50, 56, 59, 61, 71, 86 (upper photograph), 90 (lower photograph), 97 (upper photograph), 98 (upper photograph), 99, 100, 109 (upper photograph), 114 (lower photograph), 118 (upper photograph), and the colour photograph of Sydenham Park; the Price and Harrison Series for the photographs on pages 65, 67 (upper and lower photographs) and the colour photograph of the Crystal Palace Parade, c. 1905; the Horniman Museum for the photograph on page 89; the Imperial War Museum for the photographs of air-raid damage on Sydenham (74401), Cobbs Corner (1029 107351) and RAF balloon defence (CH 13906) on pages 77, 78 and 83; Lewisham Local Studies Centre for the photographs on pages 13, 16, 17, 31 (lower photograph), 33, 34, 35, 36, 46 (lower photograph), 51, 55, 60 (upper photograph), 64, 67 (lower right photograph), 72, 82, 88, 93 (lower photograph), 96, 101, 107 (lower photograph), 112, 113, 117 (middle photograph); Crystal Palace (High Level) and Catford Loop (Middleton Press) for the upper photograph on page 30; the V&A Images/Victoria and Albert Museum for the colour lithograph of the Crystal Palace by T. Picken; the governors of Dulwich College for the colour illustration of 'The High Level Station'; the National Gallery, London for the colour illustration of 'The Avenue, Sydenham'; J.D. Wetherspoon plc for the Capitol photograph on page 94; the Headteacher, Sydenham High School, for the upper photograph on page 92; the Headteacher, Sydenham School, for the lower photograph on page 92; London Borough of Lambeth, Archives Department, for the upper photograph on page 79; the illustration on the cover is reproduced by permission of Croydon Local Studies Library. All other photographs have been taken by, or are in the possession of the author.

chapter one

Early history

Very little has been found relating to prehistoric settlement in Sydenham and Forest Hill. A few Palaeolithic and Mesolithic flints were recorded without provenance and some Neolithic implements were found in the Bell Green area. It is possible that the high ridge to the west was a trackway through wooded country. Here the land rises to 350ft (105m), from where there are still extensive views which give an impression of the topography of the area before it was settled.

When Mayow Wynell Adams wrote his brief history of Sydenham in 1878, he began by saying: 'So far as I have been able to make out, Sydenham has no Ancient History. Situated at the end of the parish of Lewisham, without any direct road from London through it to any other place, it must have been, in the beginning of the seventeenth century, but a very small remote country village'. Before absorption into the Borough of Lewisham, Sydenham was in Kent and research into its early history relates to that county.

The view from the top of Sydenham Hill stretches across the clay basin in which the River Pool flows to the North Downs, rising beyond Shooters Hill. Crystal Palace Parade and Sydenham Hill follow the highest point of the ridge, giving glimpses to the west. From here it was once possible to see across London. When the poet Thomas Campbell first came to Sydenham in 1804, it was probably this view that caused him to write in a letter:

> ...the whole glory of London spread itself before us like a picture, in distant but distinct perspective. Fifteen miles and more of the peopled shore of the Thames lie in that prospect; St Paul's in the centre – Westminster towers on the left ... All the mighty idea of London enters the mind in seeing its dusky outline stretching over the whole provinces from Sydenham Hill. There lies the great city, resting its foundations on the world. The view is within a short walk of my intended home. A common, but not a naked one in the heart of the lovely country, rises all around. I have a whole field to expatiate over undisturbed; none of your hedged roads and

London out-of-town villages about me, but 'ample space and verge enough' to compose a whole tragedy unmolested.

From Sydenham Hill the land drops to a valley, towards the trackway that later became London Road. It rises to what are now the gardens of the Horniman Museum, from which are extensive views across the London basin embracing Westminster and the London Eye, the City still dominated by St Paul's Cathedral and the towers of Canary Wharf. A walk down Canonbie Road and Westwood Park reveals far-reaching views eastwards. If prehistoric people walked this area, they would have had a wide viewpoint across the surrounding land.

At that time the area was covered with woodland, which formed a barrier to settlement. Later this was known as the Great North Wood, which covered the land from Croydon to Camberwell. Remnants of this wood, mainly hornbeam and oak, are found between Sydenham Hill and College Road. The wood has been fought over in recent years to ensure its preservation because it is claimed to be much as it was over 2,000 years ago. Norwood and Forest Hill owe their names to this wood. Most of the rest of the area, later known as Westwood Common because it was in the western part of Lewisham parish, was covered with scrub and coppice. It remained generally uninhabited because of its remoteness.

There are two pieces of evidence for Romans passing through Sydenham. Excavations on allotments in 1934 revealed a slight camber suggested to be a road of tightly packed flints, 6in (15cm) deep and 20ft (6m) wide. Although doubt has now been cast on this evidence, it was presumed that the road led from the Peckham area, ascended Blythe Hill, crossed the River Pool and cut across the Downham area. From the top of Blythe Hill, where once there would have been a clear view to Roman Londinium, the direction taken by surveyors was directly in line with the Roman London Bridge and need not therefore have joined Watling Street. This was not necessarily a military road, although military engineers could have constructed it. More likely it was used by traders from the iron-working districts of the Weald of Kent and the corn-producing areas of the South Downs.

The second piece of evidence still does not indicate any settlement. In a 'gravel pit on Sydenham Common' were found part of a Roman helmet, a small coiled bronze serpent raising its head and fragments of two bronze tablets. All were presented to the British Museum in 1813. The tablets are part of a *diplomata* granted to a Roman auxiliary soldier. Until AD 212 Roman auxiliary soldiers served twenty-five years before being granted Roman citizenship. To record this, soldiers were issued with tablets bearing their record of service, the name of the provincial governor and the names of the units in which they and others who were being granted this right were serving. A married man, his wife and his children were granted citizenship; if he was unmarried, the wife of his first marriage and her children would have that right. A *diplomata* was not a discharge certificate, as is often stated, because these men could continue their military service. After AD 212 Roman citizenship automatically became the privilege of the whole empire.

The bronze serpent found on Westwood Common.

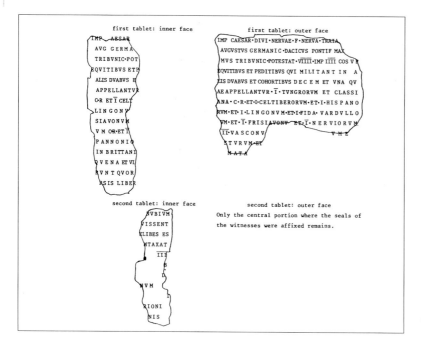

first tablet: inner face

first tablet: outer face

second tablet: inner face

second tablet: outer face
Only the central portion where the seals of
the witnesses were affixed remains.

Pieces of the Roman diplomata found on Westwood Common; Latin script.

A recent translation of the Sydenham *diplomata* has revealed that it was issued in the reign of Trajan, during the consulships of Gaius Julius Bassus and Gnaeus Afranius Dexter; that is, precisely between 4 May and 13 July AD 105. *Diplomatae* were usually issued in batches; one found at Middlewich, Cheshire and another in Moesia (a province on the Danube) were also issued at this time. Unfortunately the Sydenham *diplomata* is broken at the place where the man's name should be but we know it was granted to a man whose name ended in *nis* and who served as either a centurion or a decurion in an auxiliary cohort. Margaret Roxan, who translated the *diplomata*, suggested three possible regiments: the part-mounted First Cohort of Ligonians, stationed at Lancaster; the First Friesian Cohort, raised in the Rhineland; and the Second Mounted Cohort of Vascones, raised in the Basque Region.

For the next 1,600 years, there can only be speculation as to settlement in the area, but the lack of settlement in the early medieval period was mainly due to the presence of woodland, which restricted opportunities for agriculture. In the later medieval and early modern periods, woodland had an economic use. Oak trees were felled to provide timber for the Deptford shipyard and tannin for the leather workers in Bermondsey. Charcoal burners providing charcoal for the Surrey ironmasters and for personal cooking from the seventeenth century onwards needed a plentiful supply of wood and this implies coppicing and clearing of forest areas. The burners would take branches and pieces of wood, place them in layers and cover the whole mound with earth. The interior was fired and allowed to burn slowly, often for several days. The men lived on the site to ensure that flames would not break through the earth covering.

Clearance of the forest led to crop-growing and the keeping of sheep and cattle. Sydenham is not mentioned in the Domesday Book but Lewisham, or

Levesham as it then was, is recorded as being in the possession of the Abbot of Ghent and as having fifty hogs in the woods 'free from the pannage'. Pannage, which was 'payment for the privilege of keeping swine', allowed pigs to eat acorns in the forest and it is very likely that some roamed the Great North Wood with its plentiful supply of this food. Lewisham also had fifty villeins, nine bordars (smallholders) and three slaves. Rustics (labourers) are also mentioned. Allowing for an estimate of about sixty persons and a multiple of four persons per family, this would give a population of 240; some might have lived in isolated cottages or shelters in the Sydenham area.

The name of the area has altered frequently. It is first mentioned in AD 1206, when it was referred to as Cipeham. This became Cypenham in 1319 and Shippenham in 1315. By 1560, the name had become Sypenham. Mayow Wynell Adams states that the earliest deed of the Old House in March 1622 refers to Sidenham and yet another deed in November 1658 to Cippenham. This is shortened to Sidname in John Evelyn's diary in 1675. In 1797, Hasted stated in his *History of Kent* that the former Cypenham was now Sydenham. Ekwall, in the *Oxford Dictionary of English Place Names* of 1936, suggests that the name is akin to Chippenham, the 'S' replacement for 'Ch' being due to the Normans. Sydenham is also a place name in Oxfordshire, where it is said to derive from 'at the wide hamm', meaning a broad or extensive enclosure. Chippenham could also mean Cippa's homestead or enclosure and this could apply to Sydenham too. In *Kentish Place Names*, J.K. Wallenberg suggests that, as Sydenham is near the River Pool, the name may have derived from the root *seip*, meaning 'to let drop', which is found in the Old English *drip* or *sype* which means wetting or an act of soaking through. The 'd' replacing 'p' may be due to popular etymology. Be that as it may, by the beginning of the thirteenth century some form of settlement was sufficiently permanent to be accorded a name, even if the name varied. The name Forest Hill, on the other hand, is more recent, first being recorded in the parish register of St Mary's church, Lewisham, in 1797 and indicating the position of a hamlet in the Great North Wood.

Coppicing continued in rotation under the Abbots of Ghent and the cutting of mature trees provided timber so valuable that in 1559 Elizabeth I ordered it to be preserved for shipbuilding. Timber was carted to Deptford through the present Brockley area, probably along where Stanstead Road and Brockley Rise now run. In 1605 Henry Newport, described as 'a gentleman and yeoman of the boiling house to King James', petitioned for land on Westwood Common. Seemingly he had local knowledge of the area, and James I granted him about 500 acres. Together with other holders of leases, he began digging ditches on the Common and killing some of the cattle. This angered Abraham Colfe, vicar of Lewisham, who voiced the opposition of local people, about 100 of whom marched through the City of London to present a petition which spoke of 'five hundred poor people dependant on the common, mainly for the grazing of their animals and the collecting of fuel from the thickets'. After 'three tryalls' this petition seems to have been successful. Judgment was given to the petitioners to control enclosures and take care of the common land.

If people were grazing animals on the Common, this implies some dwellings in the area yet the centre or the main meeting point of Sydenham at that time was not the Common but probably the area of Sydenham Green, later known as Bell Green, an open space with dwellings along two sides, backed by orchards and gardens. As it was an important meeting place, there could have been an inn here, although the first one mentioned is the Bell alehouse in the 1720s, which was kept by Nicholas Stevens, son of the farming couple William and Dorothy Stevens. Five roads met at Sydenham Green. One led to Catford, which, although not lined with houses, was nevertheless an important highway because it ran along the higher slope above the River Pool to Place House, sometimes called Sydenham House or Sydenham Place House. It was named by 1331, when it was in the possession of the Abel family, as the Manor of Sydenham. In 1431 Sir John Welles, Mayor of London in that year, owned this house; the 'manor of Sippenham' is mentioned in his will of 1442.

The manor did not, however, remain in the possession of one family. Had it done so, that family could have exercised more influence in the area. The estate passed through several families until 1547, when it came into the possession of Richard Howlet, Clerk to the Navy. Given the importance of the shipyards at that time, his connections with Deptford mark his status. In his grant of arms in 1559 he is entitled 'Robert Howlet of Sidnam, Kent', which implies that he lived at Place House. Howlet's position required grandeur and he may have extended or rebuilt Place House. Engravings from the nineteenth century show a gabled house of two storeys with two protruding symmetrical sets of bow windows and an entrance porch, which extends the height of the house. A later account mentions 'spacious and lofty apartments' with glazed windows 'ornamented with the best painted glass of the times'. Howlet had no sons so on his death in 1560 the house passed to his widow, Anne, for her lifetime and then to his daughters. One daughter, Rachel, who had married Robert Edmunds, a yeoman of Lewisham, seems to have inherited but Robert had interests elsewhere. Although he and his descendants kept on the house and made use of it from time to time, they preferred to lease it out.

Amongst the tenants was the Catholic Francis Throckmorton, who was executed in 1584 for his part in a plot for a combined French and Scottish invasion of England to replace Elizabeth I with a Catholic monarch, probably Mary Queen of Scots. The Throckmorton association with Place House did not deter Elizabeth from making at least two visits. In 1590 and 1592, she descended upon Dr William Aubrey, who was then the tenant in residence, probably breaking her journey between London and Greenwich. As Elizabeth would have arrived with numerous servants, courtiers and hangers-on, these visits were always regarded with apprehension and financial anxiety. That may be the reason why, after Aubrey's death in 1595, his widow, Wilgiford, did not renew the lease. However, the next occupant, Richard Bulkeley, entertained the aged Queen in 1602, the year before her death. There is a reference to the Queen 'going a-mayenge to Sir Richard Bulkeley's at Lewisham, some three or fowre miles of Greenwich'. Since 1719 some local historians have associated this event with Honor Oak Hill, hence its name.

Subsequent tenants exercised little influence on the area. Farms and houses, such as Clare House, built for the Brooke family in around 1725, were situated alongside Perry Hill, which led from the Catford and Lewisham area to Sydenham, making use of the River Pool both for watering crops and as a source of drinking water. The road was high enough to escape flooding, while the water meadows provided lush pastures for keeping cattle. Watercress beds are detailed on early maps. Housing from the Catford area extended along the road until Bell Green and this was facilitated by the sale of land originally belonging to Place House. Housing from the Common area extended southwards. Forest Hill was yet to develop.

right Place House.

below 1778 map showing the position of Sydenham, the Common and Place House.

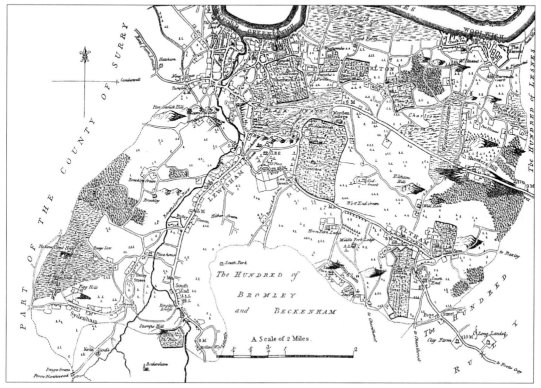

chapter two

Eighteenth-century fame

In the eighteenth century Sydenham grew in importance by exploiting the natural springs discovered in the previous century. In prehistoric and Roman times, springs were linked with healing deities who were believed to cure those who drank or bathed in the waters. The Christian Church, accepting the force of popular superstition, transmuted the deities to local saints and visits to healing wells became a popular form of devotion during the medieval period. The Protestant Reformation could not stop this but the eighteenth century, a more rational age, regarded taking the waters as a fashionable activity rather than a route to health. Spas became social amenities and society delighted in these 'watering holes'. Horace Walpole commented that 'one would think that the English were ducks! They are forever waddling to the waters'. Nevertheless there remained a belief that taking the waters alleviated pain, even if it did not provide a cure.

Over a dozen springs were noted on Sydenham Common but the main spring seems to have been in Wells Park Road, near the site of the former St Philip's church. At this point there is a split between areas of sand and clay, which allows water to trickle through. John Evelyn passed the site on 2 September 1675. After visiting Dulwich College 'in a melancholy part of Camerwell parish', he came by 'certaine Medicinal Spa Waters at a place called Sidname Wells, in Lewisham Parish, much frequented in Summer time'.

Hasted's *History and Topography of Kent* of 1778 states that the springs are 'at the foot of a hill, about twelve in number … the bottom is a loam, as is the hill, and where the water issues in, is found the *lapis lutoso-vitriolicus*, which glitters with vitriolic sparkles, and is divided into parcels by the *trichitis*'.

In 1699 Benjamin Allen described the water as being 'medicated with a salt of the nature of common salt but with a nitrous quality and a little more marcasitical'. This suggests a somewhat sulphurous taste. Hasted said that 'the water purges very quick; it is bitter, like the Epsom waters, it curdles with soap or milk'. Lysons also remarked that 'the waters resemble those of Epsom'.

A contemporary account stated they were 'a purging spring which has performed great cures in scrofulous, scorbutic, paralytic and other stubborn diseases' although it is dubious that they were 'a certain cure for every ill to which humanity is heir'. No doubt faith was required for any cure but the Sydenham springs were reputed to relieve, if not cure, rheumatism and gout.

Sydenham suffered, however, in that not all 'watering holes' were of the same rank. The most fashionable were Bath, Tunbridge Wells and Harrogate. Emulating these were numerous 'spa-lets', as they were called. In 1771 Tobias Smollett wrote: 'I am persuaded that there are fifty spaws [sic] in England … though they have not yet risen to fame: and perhaps never will, unless some medical economist should find an interest in displaying their virtues to the public view'. Smollett's 'fifty' can be doubled to provide a list of British sites which once laid claim to be fully fledged 'spaws'. London and the surrounding area had at least a dozen, with Epsom and Sadler's Wells at Islington being the most patronised, although Epsom and Tunbridge Wells denounced Islington as a 'plot', meaning a fake. Sydenham was often confused with Dulwich Wells, which were situated near to the present Harvester public house at the junction of Lordship Lane and Dulwich Common.

Daniel Defoe's *Tour through England and Wales* of 1724 indicates the lowly ranking of the Sydenham spa. Coming back from touring Surrey he passed through 'Dullige' or Sydenham Wells:

> … where great Crouds of People throng every Summer from London to drink the Waters, as at Epsome and Tunbridge; only with this difference; that as at Epsome and Tunbridge, they go for the Diversion of the Season, for the Mirth and the Company; for Gaming, or Intrieguing, and the like, here they go for meer Physick, and this causes another difference; Namely, that as the Nobility and Gentry go to Tunbridge, the Merchants and Rich Citizens to Epsome; so the Common People go chiefly to Dullwich and Stretham; and this rather also, because it lyes so near London, that they can walk to it in the Morning, and return at Night; which abundance do; that is to say, especially of a Sunday, or on holidays, which makes the better sort also decline the Place; the Croud on those Days being both unruly and unmannerly.

Indeed the clientele was not always well behaved. Hutchings, in his *London Town Past and Present* of 1909 commented that Londoners would mix 'brandy and other potent liquors with the *aqua pura*' and 'were not ashamed to impute their indisposition to this water'.

Local inhabitants sought to take advantage of the profits from the wells. Several custodians claimed ownership. One custodian, Elizabeth Fearman – known as Old Betsy – was said to be so large that when she died on 20 June 1791 'her coffin was six feet ten inches long, three feet, five inches wide and two feet six inches deep'. It is reputed that teams of men pulled the coffin on a cart to St Mary's church, Lewisham for burial, stopping at many public houses en route for refreshment. This merry party, of which Betsy would probably have approved, finally gathered round the grave for a last celebration.

Most of the wells were situated in what is now Wells Park Road and Taylor's Lane. Visitors could, as Defoe said, walk to and from London in a day but many preferred to stay the night so inns such as the Greyhound and local cottages provided accommodation and meals. There was never a large assembly hall or a public watering place such as graced Tunbridge Wells or Bath.

The fame of the wells continued throughout the eighteenth century. Hasted refers to the wells being 'discovered about 1640'. He wrote that Sippenham, now Sydenham, 'about a hundred years ago had only a few farm-houses and cottages in it, built round the common. The increase of its inhabitants, and prosperity since, has been owing to the discovery of springs of medicinal purging waters in it'. Unfortunately no analysis of the waters was made. A physician, John Peter, had commented in his *Treatise on Lewisham Waters* in 1681 that at 'the very place where now the wells are, there used to be only the gushings of water, where multitudes of pigeons used to frequent; enough to give intelligence to any observing naturalist that there was something wherewithal the water was impregnated that did invite and delight them, some saline aluminous liquor of which the fowls naturally love to be tippling'. He added that 'the water should be taken warm, either as a posset drink made in the usual way, or by mixing three pints of water with a quarter of a pint of boiling milk'.

By the nineteenth century the fame of the wells had declined. In 1878 Mayow Wynell Adams remembered the remaining well as being 'but a dirty pool and the water very nasty' and commented that the wells had been filled in. Mill Cottage, often referred to as the Green Dragon, in Wells Park Road, which was bombed in 1944, was probably the surviving reminder of this eighteenth-century phenomenon. It had a sign on top of a pole, described as a figure with the head of a dragon, two wings and a coiled forked tail. Nowadays, to remind householders of their ancient history, water pouring out from springs still gives

The Green Dragon at the Wells, home of Alexander Roberts. Sketched by Thomas Bonner, c. 1770.

problems, flooding cellars and basements. Some householders have installed automatic pumps, which switch on when the water level rises.

In their heyday the wells received visits from royalty. George III's visits coincided with military reviews on the common. *The Times* on 25 June 1792 recorded one review, noting that the King was 'attended by the Nobility and Mobility' who arrived in a great line of carriages. The Queen, the Prince of Wales, the Duke and Duchess of York and the Princesses accompanied the King and a marquee was erected to command a full view and also to provide refreshments. These were 'an elegant collation, consisting of fruits and ice' but, as the review lasted five hours, other food would surely have been provided. The King is reported to have tasted the waters, sitting for long periods protected by his Life Guards. Military and pseudo-military events were commonplace at this time. Lysons, in his *Environs of London* of 1796, mentioned that a company of archers called the St George's Bowmen, established in 1789, held archery displays at the well head. In the late eighteenth century, Sydenham had sufficient open common land to hold such events.

The Common was the site of gravel diggings and accommodated large numbers of livestock. In his 1878 memoir, Mayow Wynell Adams said:

> ... my Aunt used to tell me of a Shepherdess, by the name of Neville, dressed after the manner of a Shepherdess in a Pantomime, crook and all, with red petticoat and high-crowned pointed hat who fed her flock on the Common and drove them at night to a field at the back of the cottages opposite the 'Dolphin' public house, sleeping in a hut.

After this romantic description, it is somewhat sad to note that the shepherdess died in the Lewisham workhouse in 1814.

Pigs also roamed the area. Poet Thomas Campbell moved to Sydenham in 1804, renting a house on Peak Hill near Kinver Road. His biographer, William Beattie, commented that the poet's house, where he resided for seventeen years, stood 'on a gentle eminence, within a few minutes walk of the village, and possessed in those days the strong recommendation of a quiet, frugal and healthy retreat in a solitary part of the common'. Campbell states that one day, when standing at his door gazing at the view, he was startled 'when my wife cut short my reverie by asking if we had the right to keep pigs on the common'. As the name Peak Hill seems to have been a gentrification of Pigg Hill, he can hardly have been surprised at the pigs' presence.

Beattie described the scene from the house, with more imagination than accurate description, as being a narrow lane lined with hedgerows:

> ... from the windows the eye wanders over an extensive prospect of undulating hills, park-like enclosures, hamlets and picturesque villas shaded with fine ornamental timber; with here and there, some village spire shooting up through the 'forest', reflecting the light on its vane, or breaking the stillness with the chyme of its 'evening' bells.

The poet Thomas Campbell.

Campbell himself wrote in one letter: 'I have a whole field to expatiate over undisturbed, none of your hedged roads, and London out of town villages for me, but ample space, verge enough to comprise a tragedy unmolested'. He also spoke of nightingales being 'excessively musical around us'.

The Common was certainly used for hunting. The Fox and Hounds public house on Kirkdale is a reminder of this. The Old Surrey Hunt, which hunted on the Common, might also have met at the Greyhound, probably first built as early as 1727. The parish register of St Mary's, Lewisham records the burial in 1729 of Joseph Hide, vintner at the Greyhound. It was an obvious place to start the hunt and meet for convivial entertainment later. Some hunting dogs were kept in what were called Dog Kennel Houses. The houses stood on the corner of the present Recreation Road and Silverdale but, as labourers were reported to have occupied the site in 1766, the dogs could have been poaching.

Fairs, held on the Common until 1766, occasioned disapproval because of excessive drinking and more nefarious activities. Gypsies lived in the Great North Wood during the summer months making a living from horse-dealing, selling clothes pegs and baskets, and knife-grinding. They usually frequented the wilder parts and their haunts are commemorated in the name Gypsy Hill. Respectable members of the populace were apprehensive of their activities, accusing gypsies of pilfering and accosting travellers, especially after dark. Only when the Common was enclosed did local people feel safe. Many gypsies had by then integrated with the local community but some retained nomadic ways, returning to the area for fairs.

There were more serious concerns. Highwaymen and common footpads preyed on travellers crossing any open heathland round London. One challenged Thomas Campbell when he was walking with his wife. Campbell wrote to Sir Walter Scott in February 1805:

> ... an ill-looking man, mounted on a beautiful horse passed us. He went to both sides of the hill, came back, returned, and came back again, after looking on the road to see if it was clear. On coming close to us, he demanded our names. I spoke to him strongly at first, and threatened to call for assistance. He half dismounted – but hearing me holla to some workmen in the neighbourhood, he took his seat again and, after some incoherent expostulations with me, rode off. I got Mrs Campbell, with difficulty, home in strong fits.

The workmen pursued and captured the man. Campbell gave himself the satisfaction of 'giving him some hearty kicks, and twisting his handkerchief almost to the well-earned point of strangulation'. He felt that the man did not get his just desserts, for he notes disapprovingly that the magistrate freed him because no money was demanded. He believed that the man had discarded his pistols before he was captured, as 'there were strings about his belt, which looked like what might be supporters of fire-arms'.

Regardless of this and similar alarms, the Common provided a relaxing and recreational area for the inhabitants of Sydenham, where they could walk or take more vigorous exercise. An engraving of a view down Kirkdale shows that pleasant open spaces were visible as late as 1836, although houses and cottages are already encroaching.

Elsewhere in Sydenham, building was taking place. This was inevitable given the rise in population after the middle of the eighteenth century. Rocque's survey of 1741-45 shows that Sydenham Road, as it was later called, was scattered with small cottages and houses with spacious gardens from Sydenham Green (later Bell Green) to Pigg Hill (later Peak Hill). Linear infilling would encroach on Sydenham Road, but much of the area was still arable land, probably under plough or pasture. Mayow Wynell Adams recalls that cider was made from fruit of apple orchards. Pears were made into a drink called perry, hence the names of Perry Vale and Perry Hill.

Home Park in Sydenham Road was a substantial building. The first house on the site had been a farm dating from the sixteenth century but in 1776 Christies auctioned the land at the request of John Green Lethieullier. In the catalogue the site is described as a 'compact farm house, outhouses, garden etc. together with 18 acres of land'. The farm was rebuilt as a substantial villa ready to be rented on lease. John Rocque named another house Whagow House on his map of 1746. This was situated on the opposite side of the road from where the presbytery of St Philip Neri's church now stands. This house had also been redeveloped from a farm. Another house, Hanover Lodge, was built to the west and housed the Saunders family. Later this was also leased to a succession of tenants.

A few surviving buildings can be dated to the eighteenth century. One group is in Sydenham Road. Nos 122-124, known as The Firs, were originally one house. The building retains its severe exterior, with arched windows on the ground floor and oblong windows on the two upper floors. In 1798 it was the home of John Sutton, a livery stable keeper. The semi-detached Grove Cottage and Priory Cottage at Nos 34-36 Sydenham Road have attractive gabled volutes.

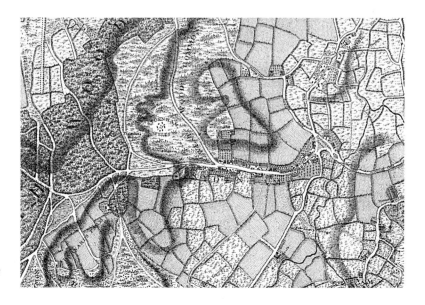

John Rocque's survey 1741-45.

The Firs, Nos 120-124 Sydenham Road, a late eighteenth-century survival. No. 120, on the right, was at one time the manse for the Dissenters' chapel.

Grove Cottage and Priory Cottage, Sydenham Road, 2004.

Sydenham was becoming a village but still straggled along the road. As to a centre, there were two possibilities, one of which is the site of the Dolphin and the Golden Lion public houses. The Dolphin dates back to at least 1733, when there is mention in the parish registers that 'Stephen, son of Richard Peke of Sipenham ye Dolphin' was buried in St Mary's churchyard, Lewisham. At this time the Dolphin was probably a farmhouse or cottage, for it was customary to sell a brew made on the premises to passers-by. In around 1790 Thomas Boxall became the landlord and built a new farmhouse behind the inn. Later this became the home farm of the Mayor family. The Golden Lion is mentioned in 1747, when John Robinson was the licensee. The presence of two public houses, so close to each other, would almost certainly form some kind of meeting area.

The second possibility is that Sydenham Green, later named Bell Green, was the centre. It was an open space at a meeting point of five roads, lined with dwellings. People usually meet around a centre of hospitality and one was available in the Bell alehouse, in use by 1729 and kept by Nicolas Stevens.

It was demolished in 1778. In 1843 another public house was built, also called the Bell, on the centre of what was originally the village green.

As well as alehouses there was at least one place of worship, the Dissenters' chapel. It was situated at the corner of the present Sydenham Road and Trewsbury Road, a road which is shown as a track on Rocque's survey. The origins of the Dissenters' chapel's are, as John Coulter says, a mystery. It may have been established by the widow of Revd John Quicke. Quicke was ejected from a living in Brixton, Devon after the Act of Uniformity was passed in 1662 and preached in London until his death in 1706. For unknown reasons, his widow 'set up the ministry of the gospel at her own charge, in a poor ignorant village, Sydenham, in Kent… unto which many wealthy citizens with their families, in the summer, ordinarily resort', according to a sermon preached at her funeral in July 1708. Rocque's survey of 1741-45 shows a 'Dissenters Meeting House' and in 1760 the Revd Mr Barron is mentioned as minister. He was succeeded by the Revd Dr John Williams in 1767. In 1777 Williams was appointed curator at the Dr Daniel William's Library, a Nonconformist library in London, although he still acted as minister until 1794 when the lease of the chapel expired. It is possible that some people attended his church not because they were Nonconformists but to avoid a muddy journey to St Mary's church in Lewisham. Those with deeper religious convictions would have felt themselves obliged to make the journey. In 1794 the church was wrenched from the Dissenters by the freeholders and was licensed for worship in the Church of England, under the name of Christ Church.

By the end of the century, the wells had declined in importance and Sydenham remained isolated. Rocque's survey shows that there were few developed roads in the area. Some houses lined the present routes of Westwood Hill and Kirkdale; fewer were in the Forest Hill area. Only a track led to Sydenham Wells. The remainder of the Great North Wood blocked development to the west. No one foresaw the developments to come.

Sydenham Road in around 1910, with the former Dissenters' Meeting House, mainly rebuilt in 1795.

chapter three

The canals and the railway: The development of commuter traffic

The canal era started in Britain in 1761 when the Duke of Bridgewater built a canal to carry coal from his mines at Worsley to the textile mills of Lancashire. The carriage of heavy goods by water was more economical than using carts passing over badly made roads. The Croydon Canal was intended to transport bulky goods from the Thames to the Channel during the French Revolutionary and Napoleonic Wars (1793-1815). Various routes were surveyed but by 1799 Ralph Dodd had suggested a route in the Kent and Surrey area from Croydon to Rotherhithe via Beckenham and running to the east of Sydenham. When this scheme was rejected because it could not accommodate large barges, John Rennie quickly replaced Dodd as consulting engineer.

Rennie proposed a route from Croydon to Rotherhithe via New Cross, Brockley, Honor Oak, Forest Hill, Sydenham and Anerley. The canal was to be 16ft (4.9m) wide at its bed and 34ft (10.4m) at the surface, with a maximum depth of 5ft (1.5m). Locks would be needed near Brockley but large barges would be able to use the canal. Its cost was estimated at £60,000. A Bill was promoted in Parliament but Dodd immediately proposed his own route for a Grand Surrey Canal, which would run westwards from Rotherhithe to Epsom, through Camberwell, Kennington and Clapham. A Bill promoting this foundered in April 1801 but, undaunted, Dodd pushed forward an amended scheme, which was passed by Parliament the next month. Money was raised and the Grand Surrey Canal, authorised initially to Epsom but with a proposed extension to Portsmouth, was begun in 1800. The company was more interested in developing the docks at Rotherhithe than in the canal and eventually it ran only 4.5 miles (7.25km) to Camberwell Road.

Meanwhile, Croydon was not to be bypassed. An Act of Incorporation was steered through Parliament in June 1801 for 'making and maintaining a navi-

The Croydon Canal and the lockkeeper's cottage near Forest Hill, c. 1815. The engraving is by H. Browne.

gable canal from near the town of Croydon…into the Grand Surrey Canal …and for supplying the towns of Croydon, Streatham and Dulwich…and the town of Sydenham with water from the said canal'. But this was not what was intended; rather the aim was to provide a navigable waterway. Eventually the problem was solved with an agreement that no water should be extracted from the canal. The canal was to join the Grand Surrey Canal at Coldblow Lane.

When the canal was completed in 1809, the cost having risen to £110,000, 'a grand cavalcade of boats' set out from Sydenham with 'barges handsomely decorated with flags'. To show commercial pretensions, the barges carried coal, stone and corn. *The Times* on 27 October 1809 noted that 'the zeal and exhilaration of the traders would not let them suffer their barges, loaded as they were, to be destitute of decoration; accordingly they all hoisted flags or streamers whatever should testify their joy that all their speculations of a profitable traffic were now realised'. In spite of this encouraging beginning, by 1811 sufficient capital could not be raised to extend the canal to Portsmouth. From 1815 the Wey and Arun Canal joining Shalford, near Guildford in Surrey, to Pallingham in Essex provided a route from London to the South Coast at Littlehampton. Even that was a commercial failure because the ending of the Napoleonic Wars destroyed a major potential source of revenue.

The amount of goods carried on the Croydon Canal was less than expected. Wharves were constructed at New Cross, Forest Hill, Sydenham, South Norwood and Penge, but the possibility of barges carrying a hundred soldiers or more quickly evaporated. The main commodities carried were timber, coal and flour. Tolls were charged for animals passing along the towpath. Horses might use it, but the company was being optimistic in expecting oxen at 8d a score and swine and sheep at 10d a score. It was also over-optimistic about the time that a barge would take to complete the full length of the canal. In summer,

passage was between 4 a.m. and 10 p.m. but in winter it was allowed only between 7 a.m. and 5 p.m. The twenty-eight locks between New Cross and Forest Hill were a problem for the bargees. Problems for the promoters were that there was leakage from the canal bed and slippage along the cuttings, especially in the Forest Hill area. The fact that the canal never went beyond Croydon was also a disadvantage and the canal was never profitable as a commercial venture.

Horses pulled the barges using a towpath mainly on the eastern bank. The path that can be seen by the side of the railway line when leaving Forest Hill station for Sydenham is a remnant of this. *Rees' Cyclopaedia* of 1819 mentions seven road- and thirty swing bridges. The bridge at Sydenham, as portrayed in engravings, seems to have been a roving bridge. These were positioned where the towpath changed sides from one bank to the other. As the horse climbed onto the bridge and crossed over the canal, the bargee lifted the rope from one shoulder of the horse to the other, thereby relieving the constant weight on one shoulder.

What the canal did successfully was to promote development along its route. Public houses were built on its banks, one being the Dartmouth Arms at Forest Hill; such was its prominence that the pub gave its name to the first railway station in that area. Other pubs, such as the Greyhound, benefited from increased custom. This was not only from the navvies who dug the canal and the bargees, but also from people seeking enjoyment. The canal was used by people sailing for leisure rather than business and in winter it was used for ice skating

The Croydon Canal at Sydenham Bridge, looking north.

and skaters would often take tea at the Dartmouth Arms and the Greyhound. Mayow Wynell Adams, whose grandfather had sold land to the canal company, remembered that 'my brothers and myself used often to hire a boat at Doo's Wharf situated near to the bridge, and row either to Croydon, or sometimes the other way to the first lock, about half way between Forest Hill and Brockley railway stations'. On Sunday afternoons they sometimes hired a four-oared boat to row to Croydon.

Angling was a popular pastime; the first licences were sold in 1814 and the canal was stocked with dace, roach and perch. Angling was also permitted at reservoirs, which were constructed along the route to ensure a constant supply of water. The reservoir at Sydenham was in the area south of Dartmouth Road and west of Kirkdale. According to Mayow Wynell Adams, the name Willow Walk (later Willow Way) comes from the row of willows 'on the margin of the water'. He and his friends used the reservoir for bathing in summer and skating in winter.

Swimming could be dangerous, so the Royal Humane Society had a lifebelt and other equipment at the Dartmouth Arms. These could not save William Bear, who tried to catch a duck that he had shot, and both lost their lives. In 1817 Tim Stollard, the landlord of the Greyhound, was accused of refusing to 'let his boat be used to save a young man who had drowned in the Sydenham Reservoir'. Stollard protested that he had not refused help; he just could not get his boat out of the boathouse on his own. The magistrates, obviously ignoring his lack of strength, disagreed. Stollard lost his licence but appealed and the licence was restored.

Another tragedy was recorded in May 1831. A young woman's body, which was found in the canal and taken to the Dartmouth Arms, was recognised as that of Mary Clark from Highgate. She had been seen wandering 'in a tearful state' along the canal, although other witnesses noted her contentedly taking tea at the Dartmouth Arms. Subsequently, when the body was discovered to be pregnant, the implication was that Mary had committed suicide but at the inquest the jury opted for a verdict of murder. If so, this was one of many unsolved tragedies for no one was ever arrested.

By the 1830s the canal's unprofitability was causing serious problems. The locks deterred most of the commercial traffic and the canal's banks were insecure, especially those at Forest Hill, which were continually slipping. Also, the railways now presented competition. In 1834 a route was proposed for a railway from London Bridge to Croydon and speculative eyes were cast on the canal route. Joseph Gibbs, who had been commissioned to make a survey of a route, recommended that it might follow or incorporate the canal route. Negotiations were opened and the canal company directors were only too willing to sell the canal for the best price they could get. By 1831 the canal system generally had peaked; 3000 miles of canals still remain today but they are almost entirely used for recreational purposes. Some canals failed entirely and were abandoned. A few were converted to roads or railway tracks, which was the fate of the Croydon Canal.

The demise of the canal was inevitable given the demand for faster transport. The growth of Sydenham and Forest Hill was part of the vast expansion of London, which was embracing the hamlets and villages in its hinterland. People commuted daily into London, enhancing both their lifestyles and the city's prosperity. Professional men from clerks to managing directors were moving to the new suburbs, relying on steam suburban railways to convey them to work. Stagecoaches served the area, stopping at public houses such as the Greyhound and the Golden Lion but their journeys could be unreliable and uncomfortable, although road traffic increased after the removal of turnpike gates.

The canal company demanded £40,000 for the canal. The board of the London and Croydon Railway offered £30,000. After intense negotiations between the principals, the bargees and a jury proposing compensation, a price of £40,250 was agreed in 1836. The enhanced price was justified because the potential for a profitable passenger service by rail was enormous, especially after the London and Greenwich Railway opened a terminus at London Bridge in 1836.

In June 1835 the railway company had got an Act of Parliament to begin building the railway and the canal was purchased in 1836 but the water was not finally drained off until 1838. The London and Croydon Railway proposed London Bridge station as the starting point of a line to Croydon via Forest Hill and Sydenham. To facilitate this, a separate station was built on the north side of London Bridge station and this opened in 1839. The railway followed the route of the canal but deviated slightly to avoid the locks north of Forest Hill, and at Forest Hill and Sydenham it went to the west of the canal.

By 1839 the railway company had built stations along the line. Sydenham retained the name of the hamlet while both Forest Hill and Norwood adopted the names of nearby public houses, being called Dartmouth Arms and Jolly Sailor, respectively. In 1845 the stations were renamed after the districts. The site of the first Forest Hill station was to the south of the present station, by the side of W.H. Smith's. The station was described as 'a neat structure of brick with dressings of stone, surrounded by a substantial wall with folding gates'. A second station was built in 1854, only to be superseded in 1883 by a handsome two-storey building in Victorian Gothic style, with arched windows and a square clock tower.

The line was formally opened on 1 June 1839 in the presence of the Lord Mayor of London, fellow directors of the Greenwich, Brighton and South East Railway Companies and 200 invited guests. It opened to the public four days later with a service of twelve trains in either direction on weekdays and eleven on Sundays. One problem was to be the line between New Cross and Forest Hill. Heavy work had been required with a cutting for 2.5 miles, as well as the removal of the locks. Vast quantities of clay were excavated, one estimate being 500,000 cubic feet (382,280 cubic metres). Some clay was used to build the embankment between Corbetts Lane and New Cross; the rest, as was customary, was spread on the top of cuttings or along the sides. This created instability, which led to slippage and falls of earth. One near Forest Hill once caused the

The entrance to the 'up' platform at Sydenham station, now demolished.

line to be closed for seventeen days. The railway company was forced to spend considerable sums flattening and strengthening the banks.

A second problem was the gradient of 1 in a 100, which meant that an additional locomotive had to be added at New Cross at the rear to push the train to Dartmouth Arms and to act as a brake on the return journey. This also necessitated sidings being constructed at Dartmouth Arms and the inconvenience of only one train an hour. To counteract this, the line was the subject of an experiment, the Atmospheric Railway, which was seriously proposed as an alternative to steam. George Medhurst, an engineer living at the end of the eighteenth century, had conducted experiments with compressed air and Henry Pinkus, an American then living in England, developed these further. In 1835 he issued a prospectus for a National Pneumatic Railway Association, which included a proposal to lay railway lines on top of roads.

The experiments attracted the attention of two brothers, Jacob and Joseph Samuda, who took the idea further in the design of marine engines. They were joined by Henry Clegg, an engineer working in Portsmouth, who suggested that their ideas might be used to improve the railway system. The scheme was patented in 1838. The Samudas and Clegg began to consider the possibility of an atmospheric railway and tried it on the London and Birmingham line at Willesden and in 1840 they were approached by the London and Croydon line to solve their gradient problem. The Samudas proposed placing an atmospheric traction on the bank which would propel sixty trains a day at 30mph (48km). These would leave at fifteen-minute intervals and, if the idea was successful, would reduce the company's costs by 20 per cent. However, the company was doubtful about the scheme so the Samudas turned their attention to Ireland, carrying out trials on the Dalkey and Kingstown Railway.

The London and Croydon Company continued to have problems, so the Samudas were approached again and in 1845 the system was finally installed. According to Edwin Course's 1962 book *London Railways*, its essential feature was:

> a continuous tube laid between the rails with a slot at the top, normally closed by a leather flap. The piston of the 'locomotive' ran in the tube, being connected to the main frame by an iron plate, which passed through the slot. When air was pumped from one side to the piston, atmospheric pressure in the other was sufficient to drive a train at considerable speed. The 15in (380mm) cast-iron tubes, laid in 10ft (3m) lengths between the rails, were spiked to sleepers through cast-iron feet strengthened by fins running underneath. Steam engines placed along the track every two or three miles worked the air pumps, which exhausted the air as the train approached and allowed it to rush in after the train had passed.

Pumping stations, in Victorian Gothic style architecture, were built at 3-mile intervals. The one at Dartmouth Arms, which was placed on the Perry Vale side of the line along with the atmospheric track itself, had a splendid chimney topped with a finial in Gothic style. It seemed more like a church than an engine house. In theory the system should have worked satisfactorily, with trains of six coaches travelling at up to 70mph. For a short time it did and passengers appreciated the silent transportation and lack of smoke. However, there were constant breakdowns with the pumping system and the leather used to form the seals was torn or eaten by rats, which were attracted by the tallow needed to soften it, leading to leakage in the tubes. Derailments occurred because of poorly laid track. The short-lived experiment ended in April 1847 when the tubes were removed. The railway company then used more powerful locomotives and by 1858 had fifty-eight trains a day running on the line.

In 1846 the London and Croydon Railway Company and the London and Brighton Company amalgamated, forming the London, Brighton and South Coast Railway Company. This increased the number of trains calling at Forest Hill and Sydenham but did not improve the service. Passengers constantly complained that trains were unpunctual, often running over an hour late. The LB&SCR was constantly mocked as being the Long-Time Blighted and Slow Coach Railway. There was also rivalry with the South Eastern Railway Company, known as the Slow, Easy and Comfortable, although comfortable was not how the passengers described it.

In 1853 London Bridge station was extended in anticipation of the heavy excursion traffic expected after the opening of the Crystal Palace at Sydenham and in 1854, to coincide with the opening of the Palace, the London, Brighton and South Coast Railway opened a branch line to Crystal Palace Low Level station. The company noted the potential profit to be made by conveying excursion passengers to the Palace and proposed running trains from Victoria. They had been forestalled in this by the London and Crystal Palace Junction Railway, which opened in 1856 with a terminus at Battersea and a line going to Crystal

Forest Hill station, *c.* 1903. The first station was situated to the right of this one.

Palace by Clapham and Balham. This had a junction with the London and Brighton line just north of Norwood. It was only a matter of time before a further amalgamation of companies used the more convenient terminus of Victoria. This not only conveyed excursion traffic to the Crystal Palace but led to the development of commuter traffic, as speculative builders turned their attention to the open land round the edges of the park.

The Crystal Palace and South London Junction Railway also noted the potential for passenger traffic and in 1862 secured the opening of a line from Peckham Rye to Crystal Palace, coming via Nunhead, Lordship Lane and Upper Sydenham (Wells Park) and terminating on Crystal Palace Hill, close to the Palace. This line opened in 1865 but profits were not as high as expected because excursion traffic was beginning to decline, although the company hoped that passenger traffic would increase if the area was developed. However, the line was never successful because it terminated at the High Level station and so did not attract through commuter traffic. Passengers from London Bridge could also alight at Sydenham and reach the lower end of the Crystal Palace Park through Lawrie Park Road. The line to the High Level station lasted until 1954 when the station was closed.

Commuter traffic in the Sydenham and Forest Hill areas greatly improved when the London, Chatham and Dover Railway obtained powers for an independent entry to stations at Cannon Street and Charing Cross, allowing passengers to gain access more easily to central London, north of the River Thames. London Bridge station was also enlarged in 1866, thus increasing its attraction as a commuter station for those who wished to live in the Sydenham and Forest Hill areas.

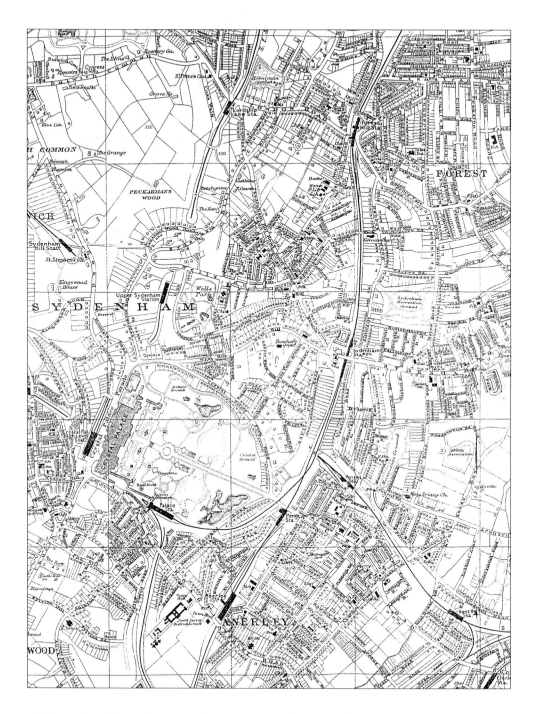

   In 1857 the Mid-Kent line opened a station near Bell Green. The station was rebuilt further west in 1906 and the line enabled passengers not only to reach the City but also the growing areas of Bromley and other Kentish towns. The Sydenham, Forest Hill and Crystal Palace areas were therefore well served for access to London and the South Coast. Builders took advantage of these improved communications by increasing the number of dwellings wherever they could.

Crystal Palace High Level station, now demolished.

View along the Croydon Railway from Dartford Arms in 1839 in a lithograph by L.J. Wood and J.R. Jobbins. The pub is part of the small group seen in the centre.

opposite Map of Sydenham and Forest Hill from 1909, showing the railway routes in the area.

chapter four

Nineteenth-century expansion

In the late nineteenth century, Sydenham and Forest Hill developed rapidly both as commuter areas and as centres in their own right. Until then, the areas could be described as pastoral. William Beattie described Thomas Campbell in 1805 as taking 'shady walks where he was safe from all intrusion but that of the Muses; enabling him to combine healthful exercise with profitable meditation'. After one visit, Sir Charles Bell wrote in his diary that he and Campbell 'rambled down the village and walked under the delightful trees in the moonlight'. Later they adjourned to the inn (presumably the Greyhound) where 'we took an egg and plotty … After breakfast we wandered over the forest, not a soul to be seen in all Norwood'. Campbell commented on the 'lovely country in my neighbourhood', where he was 'nobly settled', but he left the area in 1820 because he found the coach journey into London too expensive.

In 1839, W.E. Trotter wrote in *The Croydon Railway and its Adjacent Scenery* that the traveller, when entering the area, sees that:

> a prospect of, perhaps, the most beautiful scenery which can be found in the immediate vicinity of the metropolis suddenly opens upon us, and we feel at once the happy and enlivening influence inspired by a free communion with the pure air and light of heaven. On our left is the rich and fertile valley of the Ravensbourne, bounded in the distance by the Kentish Hills; on our right rise the woodlands of Brockley and Forest-hill, studded with villas and mansions; while immediately below us is the Dartmouth-arms station, above which the new church of Sydenham presents itself, on elevated ground beyond.

This rural and pleasing atmosphere is still apparent in the area. Pevsner, at a much later date, could remark that 'the hilly region of Sydenham has a character quite different from the rest of Lewisham'.

As late as 1851, the *Illustrated London News*, considering a possible site for the Crystal Palace after the Great Exhibition, commented, in a somewhat romantic assessment of the area, that it was a place of perfect solitude:

View down Kirkdale with
St Bartholomew's church
in the distance, 1836.

Not a sound, not an object in view betrays the close vicinity of the great city. The blackbirds and the thrushes sing away in harmonious rivalry and the rabbits dashing through the brushwood and wobbling along the fields complete the idea of a rural remote district only disturbed by the occasional thunder of a train dashing along the valley below.

The change that led to the development of the area was due to four circumstances: the enclosure of common land, the availability of land to developers, the development of the railway network and the moving of the Crystal Palace to Sydenham in 1852.

The enclosure of the common land was a consequence of the Enclosure Acts passed between 1760 and 1830, which divided up common land. In 1809, Westwood Common covered around 500 acres, extending over an area bounded approximately by the present Sydenham Hill on the west, Westwood Hill on the south, the railway line on the east and Westwood Park and Ewelme Road on the north.

The move for enclosure was led by the Earl of Dartmouth, the lord of the manor; John Forster, who had bought part of the Place House estate in 1806; and Sir Francis Baring. They brought forward a Bill in Parliament for this purpose in 1810. Their action was opposed, not least by the Mayow Adams family. William Dacres Adams had married the heiress Elizabeth Mayow in 1804. In 1878, their son, Mayow Wynell Adams, wrote about the Enclosure Act of 1810:

> The Act was passed after much opposition from some of the inhabitants, whose efforts were not as successful as those of Vicar Colfe just 200 years before … The second reading in the House of Commons being carried by a majority of only one, it so happening that my grandfather, William Adams, Esq., then MP for Totnes and another Member were shut out of the division, or the result would have been different.

Even if the vote had been different, the Act would probably not have been delayed for long because the landowners were determined to realise their assets. What happened was on a par with what was happening elsewhere in England and Wales.

When the Enclosure Act was passed in 1810, the Earl of Dartmouth received 299 acres, John Forster 71 acres and the Earl of St Germans 63 acres. The Mayow Adams family, which seemingly had lamented the passage of the Act, acquired 54 acres. After 1819, when the Commissioners' award was made, the Common was rapidly divided into plots. Those on higher ground, where it was believed the air was healthier, were bought to build large houses, some with extensive grounds, for professional people who removed to the area after the railway had been built. The houses called The Elms and The Wood were built for the Forster family, who had gained extensively from the enclosure as their building ambitions revealed. Some houses still remain on Sydenham Hill, although many were demolished after being damaged in the Second World War. Others were converted for other uses before their end; Beechwood, for example, became an International Hostel. Eliot Lodge, built on the corner of Sydenham Hill in the 1850s and later enlarged, survives to show something of its original splendour.

The second circumstance that led to the development of the area was the availability of land for developers. Westwood Common and the Great North Wood had prevented builders from moving into the area. The Croydon Canal Company prevented development by the canal and the reservoirs. Large estates

The third Earl of Dartmouth.

below The Enclosure Award Map, c. 1812.

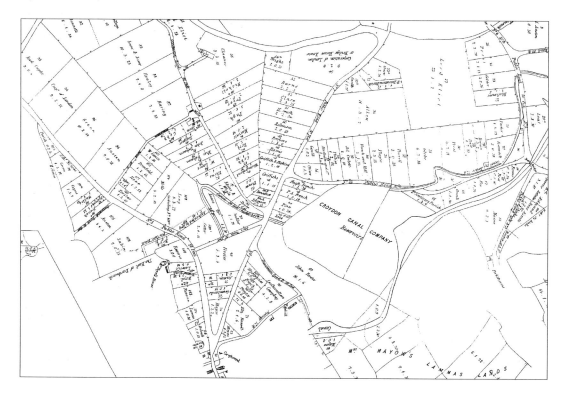

in the area, such as the Mayow and Lawrie estates, blocked large-scale development. However, once the area had begun to be enclosed, the loss-making canal company and the large estate owners began to sell their land to speculative builders eager to take advantage. The landscape gradually changed from one of large villas with spacious grounds to that of small villas and two-storey working-class houses. By 1900, the area had become almost completely urbanised with landownership continuing to fragment.

Thirdly, cheap rail transport enabled people to work in London and live in the country. By the 1860s the pattern of the railways in the area was established. London Bridge and Cannon Street stations encouraged the professional classes to commute to the city while later access to Victoria and Charing Cross enabled their families to consider a profitable day's shopping in the West End. Commuter traffic was helped by the cheap workman's ticket introduced by Gladstone in 1860, even if the train left the terminus before 5 a.m.

Fourthly, the Crystal Palace was moved in 1854 from Hyde Park and attracted further development. The Lawrie family owned an estate at the bottom of Westwood Hill, which they sold to the Crystal Palace Company in 1852. Two large buildings were already on the site: Sydenham Hall, built in 1805, which was the home of the Lawrie family, and Westwood House. Both these buildings were to survive until the next century. The former was first used to store natural history exhibits from the Crystal Palace before eventually becoming a school; it was demolished in 1939 for the building of houses in what is now Hall Drive. The latter was rebuilt in the late 1870s in Franco-Scottish baronial style for Henry Littleton, chairman of the music publishers, Novello & Company. He wished to be near the Crystal Palace because of its musical events and in his house he entertained many who performed in concerts. The house was demolished in 1952 and the Shenewood estate has taken its place.

Westwood House, first built in 1766 and largely rebuilt between 1879 and 1881. It was demolished in 1952.

The Crystal Palace Company cleared land to create Crystal Palace Park Road, giving access to the Palace and its park on the north. Houses built overlooking the park were highly prized both for the view and for their close proximity to the Palace. More land was sold to George Wythes, who owned brickworks at the point where Charleville Circus is now situated. He laid out many of the roads between Westwood Hill and Crystal Palace Park Road, building villas in the fashionable Italianate style, often set in spacious grounds. These were at first rented out but so popular was the area that demand could not keep up with supply. He then granted building leases for what was known as the Lawrie Park estate.

In 1876 James Thorne commented, 'Of old known as a genteel hamlet of Lewisham, famed for sylvan retreats, charming prospects and once for its medicinal waters, Sydenham grew rapidly after the opening of the Croydon Railway and still more rapidly after the opening of the Crystal Palace'. Mayow Wynell Adams commented: 'one result of the Palace was the purchase of the Lawrie property and the consequent building of all the homes in Lawrie Park'. Ordnance Survey maps reveal how house building crept down Westwood Hill and eventually surrounded the park.

Availability of land meant that speculative builders bought smaller plots on the lower ground. Many houses in the Kirkdale area were built of timber in weatherboarding fashion, where slats of wood are placed horizontally. Cottages built in the 1830s in Mill Gardens, so-called because it was close by a windmill, retained their pitch-covered slats until they were demolished in 1962. One survives coated in brick. Two 1820s cottages with white-painted slats survive at the junction of Kirkdale and Dartmouth Road; another two, now joined as one house, are in Mount Gardens.

The creation of Dartmouth Road led to the expansion of Forest Hill. Willow Walk, then a small lane, was widened and lined with single- or two-storey wooden houses, many lasting until the 1930s. Several houses in Kirkdale and Dartmouth Road have had single-storey shops built in front of them, as is common practice in many suburban areas. The Wells Park area was almost completely developed, with Wells Park Road being lined with small houses. Bradford Road, now demolished, had working-class housing, sturdily built with bay windows and decorative porches.

More land became available with the closure of the canal. The use of the associated reservoir only for sailing, angling and swimming was uneconomic for a railway company, hence it was drained, the debris cleared, feeder streams diverted and the area filled in. Housing development began in 1842.

Two new roads, Park Road and Albert Road (now Sydenham Park Road and Sydenham Park) were laid out. The land was bought and developed by George Allen, Robert Harrild, Thomas Hunt and William Whittle. Whittle had a brickworks (near Taymount Rise) and he supplied many of the yellow bricks for buildings in the area. Houses, often stuccoed, of three storeys, their front doors approached by elegant steps and with small balconies for first-floor windows, were spaciously planned on a regular pattern with elongated gardens

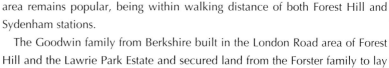

Bradford Road, c. 1905. The road was typical of many built during the expansion of Sydenham in the nineteenth century. The houses have been demolished and the street no longer exists.

Robert Harrild.

stretching behind. Many of these houses survived the Second World War. The area remains popular, being within walking distance of both Forest Hill and Sydenham stations.

The Goodwin family from Berkshire built in the London Road area of Forest Hill and the Lawrie Park Estate and secured land from the Forster family to lay out villas, in a mixture of Classical and Gothic styles, in the triangle of land between Jew's Walk, Westwood Hill and Kirkdale. William Goodwin made his intentions clear when he built a house for himself in Lawrie Park Gardens, where he and his brother George lived and worked. The Goodwins were influenced by Charles Barry, the eldest son of Sir Charles Barry who had built the Palace of Westminster. Barry, who may have lived for a time in Sydenham Park, favoured the Italianate style and probably influenced the decoration on many of the buildings in the area.

Although houses in the area have been destroyed and altered, some still survive to give a glimpse of their former splendour. One of the best is The Old Cedars, at the bottom of Westwood Hill, which is now a care home. Its position, standing back from the road, emphasises its former importance. It still retains a rear part dating from 1790 and a wing built in 1870. Another house is Sunnydene with its elaborate Queen Anne decoration, at the corner of Sydenham Hill. It was built in 1868 by J.F. Bentley, architect of Westminster Cathedral, who also built Elleslie adjoining Sunnydene. Both were built for W.R. Sutton, founder of the Sutton Housing Trust.

Further developments in the area followed quickly, as if its potential was now realised. The Forster family offered the remainder of their Sydenham Common land for building leases and Longton Grove and Longton Avenue, to the north of Jew's Walk, were laid out after 1857. The proximity of the Crystal Palace led to

York Villas, Sydenham Park.

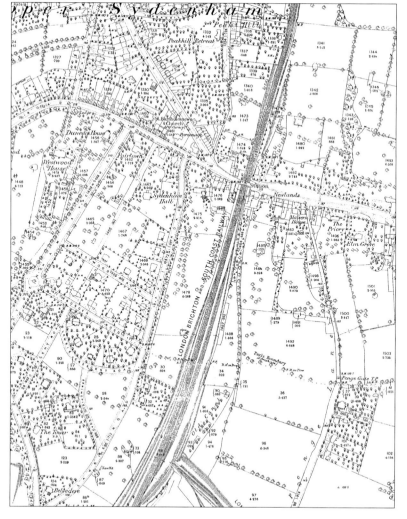

This map of 1871 shows the expansive layout of the large houses surrounded by extensive grounds.

Newlands Park, *c.* 1906.

building on Sydenham Hill. The governors of the Dulwich College estate authorised the felling of parts of Dulwich Wood, emphasising that the plots available were in the 'immediate neighbourhood' of the Crystal Palace. Mention of their closeness to Gipsy Hill station seems to have been an afterthought. The governors, with an eye to their own educational establishment, offered places at the college for the sons of those who leased plots or commissioned houses on this land.

In 1880 the Newlands estate was sold, and the last open area between Sydenham and Penge was covered with houses. The Leathersellers' Company demolished its eighteenth-century terrace of houses in Peak Hill and replaced them with 'fashionable villas'. One of the demolished houses was that where Thomas Campbell had lived. Tempted by what was going on, the Mayow Adams family had sold the northern part of their land in the 1860s for what was to be called South Sydenham Park, but development there was far more slow and irregular. This did, however, enable Mayow Road to be constructed from Sydenham Road to Forest Hill, thus opening up the area. Mayow Wynell Adams reported that 'The road cost a very large sum and is not only a pretty drive, but a great advantage to the public as it saves half a mile between Sydenham and Forest Hill'.

The family also responded to a plea from the Reverend William Taylor Jones, principal of Sydenham College, to create a 'Public Recreational Ground'. They sold 17½ acres for £8,500; the Metropolitan Board of Works contributed £4,250 after getting permission from Parliament; £1,000 was contributed from the Lewisham Parochial Charities and £3,250 was collected by public subscription. The Lewisham Board of Works agreed to take charge of its upkeep, allowing Mayow Wynell Adams to comment that it was 'the prettiest Public Park in the Metropolis'. He hoped that it would 'be a source of pleasure and health for

Sydenham Recreation
Ground, now Mayow Park,
c. 1900.

all succeeding generations in Sydenham and Forest Hill'. When Mayow Park finally opened in 1878, in the presence of a crowd estimated to number 10,000, it was declared to be 'open and free for ever'.

The Earl of St Germans promoted building in Forest Hill using his family name of Eliot to create Eliot Bank and St Germans Park (now Honor Oak Park) in the 1850s. The Earl of Dartmouth, who had received 299 acres of the enclosed land, seems to have developed his plots more slowly. Dartmouth Park in Forest Hill was developed around the new Christ Church, on a site given by the earl in 1834, probably in an attempt to make the area more fashionable. Public subscription to build the church proved so difficult that work was not started until 1850.

The Earl allowed Thomas Parker, a Lewisham solicitor, to receive some of the land and in turn Parker sold this to William Beck, a Middlesex cheese merchant. Beck built Prospect Villas, two three-storey houses with basements, on London Road near Forest Hill station. Other builders, including William Goodwin, added to his development. These houses had large elongated back gardens and substantial front gardens. A distinctive pattern emerged as some smaller houses for servants or city clerks were built on the opposite side of London Road and on the other side of the railway line, which soon became regarded as a working-class area. Devonshire Road was developed with medium-sized houses and gardens, intended for lower middle-class families, where the main occupation was city clerk or shop assistant. Forest Hill was being developed as quickly as Sydenham but there was less interest in building large houses in spacious grounds.

Basic services were needed to supply the growth in population. As late as 1843 Sydenham residents were reported to be still getting water from the River

Christ Church, Forest Hill, now converted into housing.

40

Pool, wells and from water sellers, who delivered water to the houses in huge casks, many of them filled from a deep well on Peak Hill. In 1804 Thomas Campbell had bought his water from this well at a cost of two shillings a barrel, an excessive sum at a time when labourers' wages were five shillings a week. The flow from this well lessened when the Crystal Palace Company dug its own wells but it continued to supply water until the Lambeth Water Company established a system of mains from the top of Sydenham Hill in 1857, which enabled water to be supplied to Forest Hill and Sydenham. It was not until 1903, however, that the Metropolitan Board of Works ensured a constant water supply.

In 1849 the Metropolitan Commissioners of Works produced a plan for the disposal of sewage, as there were complaints about the state of privies, cesspools and offensive drainage. Sydenham sewage was discharged into the River Pool and was therefore the cause of bouts of illness. The smell in hot weather must have been revolting. It was another seven years, however, before the Lewisham Board of Works provided some decent sewerage facilities. Lighting and fuel was also a problem; not until 1853 did the North Surrey Gas Company become established in Bell Green and begin to install gas fittings. The next year it became the Crystal Palace District Gas Company and moved to its present site. By 1858 gas lamps had been installed in the streets. In 1891 the Crystal Palace District Electric Light Company was established in Wells Park Road. Sydenham and Forest Hill relied on the Crystal Palace for many services. They utilised the Palace's volunteer fire service until the London County Council provided a fire brigade in Perry Vale in 1901.

The effort devoted to material improvements in the area was matched by the provision of spiritual help in the nineteenth-century tradition. In the eighteenth century there had been one religious establishment, a Dissenters' Meeting House. To obtain the benefits of the Anglican Church, parishioners had to travel to St Mary's church, Lewisham or St George's church, Beckenham. A new church in Sydenham was seen as vital. Mayow Wynell Adams' history says that in 1824 his father, William Dacres Adams, wrote to the Bishop of Oxford, who was also vicar of Lewisham, pointing out that, in spite of the increase in population, 'the Hamlet of Sydenham was entirely destitute of any place of worship, except Mr French's chapel, now Christ Church, where the seats were very expensive and where there were no free sittings'. He requested that the Church Building Commissioners should be asked to raise funds to erect a church and said that they should also create a separate parish for the area. Adams sought the help of the Earl of Dartmouth, who expressed his approval.

It was agreed that the growth in population – Mayow Wynell Adams calculated that the population of Sydenham and Forest Hill was then around 1,700 – demanded the addition of a new church. One problem was finding a site. After considerable negotiations, the Forster family offered part of their land to the Church Commissioners for £600. With some relief, the Commissioners accepted this offer and appointed Lewis Vulliamy, a noted church architect, 'to commence the works without delay'. Building began in 1829 but almost immediately there were problems with the foundations. Eventually Vulliamy had to make the foundations about 20ft deep, at a cost of £4,000. There were various other problems, which so infuriated Samuel Forster that he threatened to take back the land that he had given for the church and the churchyard. It took all the diplomacy of William Dacre Adams to induce the Church Commissioners to resolve the disputes. The delays meant that St Bartholomew's church was not finished until 1832. It cost £11,086 and the Commissioners provided all the money by means of a parliamentary grant. Samuel Forster, now mollified, presented the church clock. Pevsner describes the church as being made of 'stock brick. W[est] tower with thin buttresses and straight-topped diagonal pinnacles'. Edwin Nash added an apsidal chancel in 1858. The roof was raised and the clerestory windows enlarged. The church was enlarged between 1874 and 1882 by adding a north aisle and a choir vestry, while the decoration was enhanced with carved capitals on the interior columns.

St Bartholomew's church is depicted in a painting by the French Impressionist artist Camille Pissarro. Pissarro came to England in December 1870 to escape the Franco-Prussian War, remaining until he felt safe to return in June 1871. His relatives in South London arranged lodgings in the Norwood area. Pissarro made at least thirteen paintings during his stay in England, including some of the Crystal Palace. Two, possibly three, were painted in Sydenham. The most famous is 'The Avenue, Sydenham', which shows Lawrie Park Avenue looking towards St Bartholomew's church. This was done in 1871 and, somewhat surprisingly, the view can easily be recognised today. The small white posts lining the route have gone – to see something similar one needs to go to Dulwich Village – and the horse-drawn cab has been replaced by cars. Modern houses line the road but the white house at the end on the left is still there. In 1984 the National Gallery bought the painting for £560,000.

In the same year as he painted 'The Avenue, Sydenham', Pissarro made a watercolour of the scene, simplifying it by omitting the horse-drawn cab. He also produced a watercolour entitled 'Lawrie Park Gardens', which is now in the Louvre in Paris. It included the gabled end of Lethen Grange, which was demolished in 1954. While 'The Avenue, Sydenham' is painted in gentle pastel shades, 'Lawrie Park Gardens' is painted in a far more dramatic style with russet colours dominating. Another painting of the area, 'Lordship Lane Station, East Dulwich', is in the Courtauld Institute in London. It shows the railway line leading to the High Level station at Crystal Palace. A train puffs its way between green banks with Lordship Lane station in the middle distance.

On Sunday 30 March 1851 the first and last official religious census took place in Britain. Some clergymen flatly refused to allow this census to be taken, believing that it was an insult to God, and it has never been repeated. The census was intended to indicate that more churches were needed for a growing religious population. In the event it proved that, on the whole, there was adequate church accommodation. The census nonetheless revealed that there were few churches in Sydenham and none in Forest Hill. The population then was

St Bartholomew's church, 1917. In front is a military ambulance, possibly for the needs of soldiers billeted in the area at that time.

4,501, with the number of inhabited houses being 801 and twenty-eight under construction. The number of sittings in St Bartholomew's church was 900. It had a respectable morning congregation of 470 adults and 193 children, an after-noon attendance of 225 adults and 193 children and an evening congregation of 245. The Episcopal chapel in Lower Sydenham, which was later called Christ Church, had a total of 540 sittings. It had a morning congregation of 400, an afternoon one of 150 and 250 for what it describes, surprisingly for March, as an 'evening in summer'. The Independent Park chapel in Sydenham Park raised a morning total of 151 and an evening one of 120. The Independent chapel in Wells Road, with seating for 190, was only a third full with forty-three in the morning and 35 in the evening. This was reported to have 'No Sabbath School'. It was not surprising that it closed shortly afterwards. The Wesleyan chapel erected in 1849 reported a total of 123 at the morning service and eighty-two in the evening. The churches were on average less than half full but this did not deter the Anglican Church from building new ones, and the Nonconformists and Roman Catholics were to follow. The opening of the Crystal Palace and the consequent growth of Sydenham stimulated this activity.

In 1902 Richard Mudie-Smith undertook a survey in the London area for the *Daily News*, as he believed that the 1851 census had not been taken correctly and that it was out of date. He recruited 400 enumerators, mostly army and navy pensioners, to work through London, borough by borough. They would stand at the door of a church 'neatly dressed' and 'respectfully' count every person who entered. This took a year, from November 1902 to November 1903. The enumerators found that, contrary to what several clergymen had

DAILY NEWS SURVEY 1902-1903:: TOTAL ATTENDANCE FOR SYDENHAM AND FOREST HILL									
Churches	Morning				Evening				Total of day
	Men	Women	Children	Excel total	Men	Women	Children	Excel total	Excel total
Christ Church, Forest Hill	92	208	142	442	132	295	104	531	973
St Paul's, Forest Hill	68	147	61	276	86	168	43	297	573
Holy Trinity, Sydenham	97	207	90	394	55	116	21	192	586
St Bartholomew's, Sydenham	119	378	151	648	103	302	60	465	1113
St Matthew's, Sydenham	55	129	122	306	61	168	53	282	588
Christ Church, Lower Sydenham	61	110	121	292	55	112	64	231	523
St Philips, Sydenham	86	235	130	451	53	192	51	296	747
St Michael's and All Angels, Sydenham	38	43	149	230	27	64	24	115	345
Holy Trinity Mission, Forest Hill	0	0	0	0	10	33	42	85	85
St Michael's, Bell Green	2	1	100	103	10	24	30	64	167
High Street Methodist Church, Sydenham	67	82	81	230	105	161	54	320	550
Wesleyan Chapel, Sydenham Road	25	22	24	71	23	37	33	93	164
Primitive Methodist Chapel, Forest Hill	38	27	74	139	42	66	32	140	279
Trinity Methodist New Connexion, Forest Hill	36	41	45	122	41	90	25	156	278
Sydenham Baptist Chapel, Forest Hill	58	92	75	225	80	132	27	239	464
Zion Baptist Chapel, Forest Hill	27	24	14	65	23	39	8	70	135
Perry Rise Baptist Chapel, Sydenham	69	87	174	330	54	118	51	223	553
Congregational Church, Sydenham	73	85	59	217	47	86	20	153	370
Queen's Road Congregational, Forest Hill	32	37	7	76	33	70	8	111	187
Park Hall Congregational Mission, Sydenham	5	5	70	80	0	0	0	0	80
Devonshire Road Presbyterian, Forest Hill	178	211	129	518	112	172	33	317	835
Ewart Road Presbyterian, Forest Hill	4	2	223	229	25	64	92	181	410
Mayow Hall Brethren, Sydenham	29	45	14	88	32	63	16	111	199
German Protestant Church, Sydenham	57	65	16	138	9	48	1	58	196
Bible Christian Church, Stanstead Road	38	39	43	120	49	62	18	129	249
Salvation Army, Forest Hill	13	6	12	31	21	38	52	111	142
Our Lady and St Philip Neri R. C., Sydenham	79	192	90	361	36	100	29	165	526
London City Mission, School of Art, Sydenham Hill	0	0	0	0	6	26	4	36	36
London City Mission, Willow Walk	9	7	100	116	7	17	33	57	173
Grand Total	1455	2527	2316	6298	1337	2863	1028	5228	11526
Excel total	1455	2527	2316	6298	1337	2863	1028	5228	11526
error	0	0	0	0	0	0	0	0	0
Denomination									
Church of England	618	1458	1066	3142	592	1474	492	2558	5700
Weslyan Methodist	92	104	105	301	128	198	87	413	714
Primitive Methodist	38	27	74	139	42	66	32	140	279
Methodist New Connexion	36	41	45	122	41	90	25	156	278
Baptist Church	154	203	263	620	157	289	86	532	1152
Congregational Church	110	127	136	373	80	156	28	264	637
Presbyterian Church	182	213	352	747	137	236	125	498	1245
Brethren	29	45	14	88	32	63	16	111	199
German Church	57	65	16	138	9	48	1	58	196
Salvation Army	13	6	12	31	21	38	52	111	142
Roman Catholic Church	79	192	90	361	36	100	29	165	526
Other Services	47	46	143	236	62	105	55	222	458
Grand Total	1455	2527	2316	6298	1337	2863	1028	5228	11526

Church attendance numbers for Sydenham and Forest Hill, extracted from the *Daily News* survey, 1902.

said in 1851, the weather made no difference to people's church attendance. The census did reveal an increase in the number of churches, especially those belonging to the Nonconformists.

The attendance figures look respectable. St Bartholomew's church had a morning attendance of 478, with 151 Sunday school children; an afternoon congregation of 225, with a Sunday school of 193; and an evening congregation of 465. This was better than Christ Church, Forest Hill, where the morning congregation was 290 adults and 142 children but a more pleasing 427 adults and 105 children in the evening. The Congregational church in Jew's Walk had a morning congregation of 158 adults and 69 children and an evening one of 133 with 20 children. The Congregational church in Queen's Road, Forest Hill had a morning congregation of 69 with only 7 children and an evening one of 103 and 8 children. The St Philip Neri church raised 271 adults and 90 children for morning Mass and 136 and 29 children for Vespers. The majority of the adults were women. Overall it appeared that Nonconformity was not as strong in the south of England as it was in the north where Nonconformist congregations were much larger.

Christ Church in Forest Hill was consecrated in 1854. It was a Gothic cruciform structure with an apsidal chancel and was described as being one of the handsomest churches in the neighbourhood. At the same time, this church and St Bartholomew's church in Sydenham were made into separate parishes. Ten years later it was proposed to establish a chapel of ease in Wells Park Road. This resulted in the building of St Philip's church, which was opened in 1866, in the same year that Holy Trinity church in Sydenham Park was built. St Michael and All Angels' church was built in Lower Sydenham in 1864 and the so-called 'iron church' in Panmure Road was demolished to allow St Matthew's church to be built in 1880. This was never fashionable as it began as a mission to the poor but by the end of the century it had attracted a middle-class congregation. The Dissenters' chapel, now Anglican and known as Christ Church, had had problems in 1813 when the roof had fallen in. This was repaired and further major repairs took place in 1845 when a small spire was added. In 1873 it became a chapel of ease to St Michael's church.

The Nonconformists were also active. The Congregationalists in Sydenham, who had had a chapel in Sydenham Road since 1819, inherited those Dissenters who had broken away from the Dissenters' chapel in 1794. The congregation was continually split by faction, which may account for the low attendances recorded in the religious census. In 1850 they turned the building into a school and built a chapel in Sydenham Park, moving ten years later to a new chapel at the end of Jew's Walk. This occupied a prominent site until it was demolished in 1973. St John's Presbyterian church in Forest Hill began in 1870 in Frederick Horniman's house before it moved to the Sydenham Lecture Hall. In 1882 a new church was built. The Baptists established a chapel in Dartmouth Road and the Strict Baptists opened one at the corner of Perry Vale and Perry Rise. The Wesleyan Methodists built Wesley Hall in Sydenham Road and a chapel in Dartmouth Road; the Primitive Methodists had a chapel in Forest Hill. The Quakers had a meeting house on the corner of Venner Road. An Independent meeting house was established in Mayow Road.

right St Philip's church, Taylor's Lane. It was built between 1865 and 1867, damaged in the Second World War and demolished in 1982.

below One statue survives from Holy Trinity church, Sydenham Park, which was demolished in 1981.

The Sydenham Congregational church, Jew's Walk, which was built in 1867 and demolished in 1873. On the corner is the drinking fountain commemorating Queen Victoria's Golden Jubilee in 1897.

Church of Our Lady and St Philip Neri, built in 1882 on the corner of Watlington Grove and destroyed by bombing in 1940.

The Roman Catholics had been established since 1852 at St Mary's Oratory, a country retreat for the priests of Brompton Oratory on Sydenham Hill. In 1872 Bishop Danell of Southwark decided to open a mission in Sydenham. A priest, Father Augustus Bethell, bought a house in Sydenham Road as a presbytery and opened a small chapel at the side. In 1874 a school was opened which soon became popular. In 1887 Father Bethell bought a small piece of land at the corner of Watlington Grove as a site for a permanent church. He was then transferred to Anerley so his successor, Father William Addis, raised funds to build the church, which was consecrated in 1882 as Our Lady and St Philip Neri church. This was a plain building with a thin spire at one end; the nave was extended in 1912.

Towards the end of the century, Sydenham attracted a number of Germans, including the Consul General, Dr Von Bojanowski. This may have been due to Sydenham's proximity to Crystal Palace and its musical life, for conductor

The German Evangelical church in Dacres Road was built in 1883 and destroyed in the Second World War.

August Manns and many of the orchestra at the Palace were German. The 1891 census noted 233 Germans in Forest Hill. There was a German high school in Wood Vale and a preparatory school in Manor Mount. Sydenham also attracted merchants, traders and clerks from the City, and refugees from the revolutions in Germany. In 1875 services in German were held in the Lecture Hall at Sydenham and soon an appeal for funds raised enough money to buy a site and build a church. The German Evangelical church, a Gothic building with a tall spire, was built in Dacres Road in 1883.

To match the spiritual provisions in the area, new public houses were built, although many seem to have been beer houses. In the middle of the nineteenth century, there were about fifty pubs in Sydenham and Forest Hill but many lasted only briefly. Some bore exotic names such as the Cottage of Content in Wells Park Road. Others were breweries and the Brewery Tap flourished in Lower Sydenham from 1870 to 1917. The Dartmouth Arms quickly took advantage of the custom brought by the Croydon Canal by establishing a tea garden; soon it turned its attention to supplying refreshment to railway workers and commuters. The long-established Greyhound catered for the navvies who built the canal and the workers on the railway.

In 1859 Sydenham had a spurt of patriotism. In spite of Napoleon III siding with Britain in the Crimean War (1853-56), the British were constantly worried that the French might invade. Volunteer forces were raised and many people were able to display their military ardour. The Armoury, a building at the junction of Perry Vale and Hindsley's Place, served as the headquarters of

SYDENHAM. — The Station.

The Greyhound public house. To the right is the entrance to the up platform of Sydenham station.

the Sydenham and Forest Hill patriotic volunteer force, initiated as a result of a meeting called on 29 June 1859 by John Scott Russell, who built the *Great Eastern* iron steamship. A firing range was provided by William Dacres Adams on the east side of the railway between Forest Hill and Sydenham stations. The satisfaction felt by Mr Adams at his patriotic gesture was short-lived; within a few months he was complaining about the safety of the range and the intrusion of firing butts to prevent stray bullets. The Armoury housed the weapons of what had become the Sydenham Rifle Corps, eventually numbering sixty volunteers. By December 1860 it had been renamed the 8th Kent Rifle Volunteer Corps. It existed, like many other volunteer and yeomanry corps, as a social club until it was disbanded in 1871.

Education was also a concern in the nineteenth century. The Anglican and the Nonconformist churches established elementary schools in order to educate poor children. St Bartholomew's church founded a National School in 1832, the year the church was consecrated. This school, on the corner of Kirkdale and Sydenham Park, was rebuilt in 1862. Christ Church, Forest Hill opened a school in 1859. In 1870 William Forster's Education Act declared that districts should elect School Boards, which would arrange for schools to be built where there was inadequate provision. A London Board School was quickly established but this secular move galvanised the Anglican Church to increase its educational activities. National Schools were provided by St Michael and All Angels' church in 1872, St Philip the Apostle's church in 1873 and Holy Trinity church in 1874. Mrs Victoria Smith (née Cabellero) opened a school for Catholic children in a house in Wells Park Road in 1870 but it was not until 1892 that a permanent Catholic school was established in Watlington Grove.

The London School Board opened Sydenham Hill School in Forest Hill in 1874. It took over the British and Foreign School housed in part of the Sydenham Lecture Hall, a building constructed in 1861 as a Working Men's Institute to the designs of Paxton. Haseltine Road School was established in Lower Sydenham in 1882. In addition, there were schools for orphaned and abandoned children. In 1873 the Forest Hill Industrial Home, founded as one of the Earl of Shaftesbury's homes 'for the reception and training of destitute boys', began in Rojack Road. The boys were educated at Christ Church School and learned a trade, the majority in shoemaking. Ten years later, the home moved to Shaftesbury House, Perry Rise. A Girls' Industrial Home was founded in 1881, also in Rojack Road, and ten years later was occupying Louise House in Dartmouth Road. The girls, as was to be expected at this time, were trained for domestic service. Both these schools seem to have been invited to make regular visits to Frederick Horniman's museum collection at Surrey House. Part of Sydenham Lecture Hall was converted into a technical college when London County Council made full use of the fact that the duty put on beer and spirits by the Local Taxation Act of 1890 could be used to fund technical education. People who could afford the fees sent their boys to Dulwich College, Colfe's School or one of the schools in the City of London. There were a number of private schools, many short-lived. Some schools utilised large houses which were sold when a family died out or left the area. These included Sydenham Hall, which became 'a first-class preparatory school for the sons of gentlemen', and Strathmore College in Sydenham Park for 'young ladies'. Some were purpose-built like Stone House in Honor Oak Rise, which housed 'Dr John Morgan's Forest Hill School for Young Gentlemen', and Sydenham College built in 1856 specifically as a boy's college, which was run by the dynamic Revd William Taylor Jones. The 1856 prospectus noted that 'the system of education is founded on the cultivation of religious and moral principles' and that the school was in a 'delightful salubrious locality'.

The emphasis was on gentility. Campion House School and Caen Tower advertised themselves as being for the daughters of gentlemen. Rocklea College in Hillcrest Road, which educated the sons of gentlemen, was in the capable hands of Elizabeth Parry; and the Revd John Botheras ran Stafford College in Westbourne Road. The proliferation of schools may explain why there is a clause in the leases of many houses indicating that the house is not to be used for a private school. Most schools, however, had closed before the First World

The former Sydenham Lecture Hall, built to Paxton's designs in 1861, now the Kirkdale Learning Centre.

Sydenham High School,
c. 1900.

War, with 1912 being a particularly bad year for closure. One that remained open was Tudor Hall School, run by the Revd and Mrs Todd. John Todd had come to Sydenham to minister to a group of Baptists and raised the money to build a chapel. He had founded a school in Salisbury in 1850 as a select establishment for young ladies and this was continued in the Todds' house in Perry Hill in 1855. It moved to the Red House, a mock-Tudor house in South Road in 1865. The school widened the curriculum, arranged teaching by visiting professors and took advantage of the Crystal Palace and the locality of London to make educational visits. In 1908 the school moved to Chistlehurst and then, during the Second World War, to Burnt Norton near Chipping Camden. After the war, it removed to Banbury.

The Girls' Public Day School Trust opened Sydenham High School in 1887. The trust was a company set up in 1872 to ensure that girls were given the same liberal education as boys. The Sydenham school was established as a result of an appeal by a Mr Chadwick, then living in Highbury, who felt that there should be a school for girls in this area of London. The school opened in the former Longton Hall Hydropathic Hotel on Westwood Hill, between Taylor's Lane and Longton Grove. The house was quickly adapted, the large Turkish bath in the basement becoming a cloakroom and bicycle shed and the bedrooms being turned into classrooms.

Children benefited in another capacity. In 1872 Mr and Mrs Edmund Chapman and Mrs Chapman's sister, Edith Elwes, opened a small home for sick children in Kent House Road. This philanthropic gesture did not please their neighbours, whose vociferous objections persuaded them to move. Nos 5-6 Albion Villas Road were bought and opened as a hospital for sick children. It later became Sydenham Children's Hospital in Sydenham Road and was an invaluable addition to the community.

By the 1870s growth in the area had slackened. Most available land had been built on and further development was a matter of infilling as, for example, when the Mayow Adams estate was sold. The character of Sydenham and Forest Hill had also been defined. In *Life and Labour of the People of London*, Charles Booth cast a shrewd eye upon what had become a suburb of London. He noted that more well-to-do people lived mainly in the Upper Sydenham area and the higher parts of Forest Hill, where houses were set in 'well-wooded gardens'. These people employed servants, who might not necessarily live on the premises. In the Wells Park Road and Perry Hill areas, the middle class lived amongst builders, shop assistants and clerks, who found Sydenham and Forest Hill convenient areas for commuting to the City. The working class lived in Lower Sydenham and Bell Green, where small terraced houses had small gardens. Many men were 'gas workers of all kinds, porters, jobbing gardeners, road men and casual labourers, working class almost exclusively and excessively poor. Ninety per cent would feel the pinch of a week's loss of wages'. In Forest Hill there were a few 'poor and crowded streets', but Bell Green was 'the one really poor district in this quarter of London'. The framework of streets and housing had been defined and was not altered until the dramatic changes brought about after the Second World War.

Sydenham Children's Hospital.

chapter five

The life and death of the Crystal Palace

In August 1852 there was intense activity on Sydenham Hill. 550 tons of wrought iron, 350 tons of cast iron and 400 tons of glass were conveyed up the hill by two-horse drays, and 6,400 workmen converged on a site at its top. Before the disbelieving eyes of spectators, a building of iron and steel gradually arose, while 200 acres of land stretching down the eastward slope were transformed into a park. The vast structure led to the extension of the village of Sydenham and gave its name to the area – the Crystal Palace was being constructed.

Its origins went back to 1847. The Victorians were tireless in exploring the boundaries of the possible and made many advances, including a revised transport system, an expansive building programme and a futuristic use of materials such as iron and steel. It was also an era that gloried in enterprise and the promotion of British industry. The products of Britain and her vast Empire were best displayed in exhibitions. Three small exhibitions had been held between 1847 and 1849, under the auspices of Sir Henry Cole, then an assistant keeper at the Record Office. Cole was a polyglot associated with the founding of the Penny Post, a writer, music critic and painter. He was perhaps best known as the publisher of the first Christmas card and was passionately interested in industrial design. In 1849 he visited the Paris Exhibition. The French had promoted exhibitions since the end of the eighteenth century and Cole was impressed by the size and magnificence of the exhibitions and particularly with their incorporation of the products of the French Empire. Why should Britain not outdo France by exhibiting the vast range of goods from Britain's much larger Empire?

For this project, Cole needed a site, a building and, above all, a patron. This last was immediately available. Queen Victoria's husband Prince Albert, frustrated by being kept out of English politics, had turned his attention to social reform and artistic endeavour. Wishing to ally arts and sciences, he had become president of the Society of Arts and had taken a leading role in promoting the exhibitions of the 1840s. Cole had already suggested to the Prince that a larger exhibition could be held in 1851. Enthused by his visit to Paris, Cole suggested that the next exhibition should be international. Prince Albert proposed Somerset House as a venue but an international exhibition needed more space. Cole thought Hyde Park would be ideal; the Prince agreed. In a speech at the Mansion House on 21 May 1850, the Prince laid out his ideals for a Great Exhibition:

> Gentlemen, I conceive it to be the duty of every educated person closely to watch and study the time in which he lives, and, as far as in him lies, to add his humble mite of individual exertion to further the accomplishment of what he believes providence to have ordained.

Later that year he accepted the post of president of the Board of Commissioners.

So great was his enthusiasm that the board included the Prime Minister, Lord John Russell, Sir Robert Peel, William Gladstone, Richard Cobden and Robert Stevenson. A firm of constructors, James and George Munday, said that they would finance the whole scheme provided that they were ensured of two-thirds of the total receipts. Although a contract was signed, Prince Albert's ideal was for a non-commercial scheme so that people would feel that the exhibition belonged to them. The board therefore decided to raise money by public subscription and by the end of 1850 over £70,000 had been raised and the Mundays compensated for revocation of contract.

What was needed next was a builder. In January 1851 the Building Committee was formed. They asked for designs for a temporary, easy-to-construct building and 245 plans arrived. This overwhelmed the committee, which announced it could not choose any of them. They then proposed their own plan, which was met with an outcry by the press, not surprisingly as it was both ugly and in defiance of the committee's own specifications, being partly built of brick and therefore not a temporary structure. A huge dome, which had been suggested by Brunel, the railway engineer, topped a long building, with a large entrance at one end flanked by two small ones on each side. Public reaction to the idea of an exhibition being held in Hyde Park was so hostile that the whole project was almost dropped. However, the Foreign Office had become enthusiastic for foreign participation and, at the last moment, a saviour emerged.

Joseph Paxton, the seventh son of a farm labourer, was born in 1803 at Milton Bryant in Bedfordshire. This was part of the Duke of Bedford's estate, and it was here that Paxton was introduced to horticulture. Seventh sons are said to flourish and Joseph certainly did. By the age of twenty-one he had become under-gardener at the sixth Duke of Devonshire's London villa of Chiswick House. The so-called Bachelor Duke, impressed with his talent, promoted him to be head gardener at Chatsworth. According to legend, Paxton took the coach from London to Chesterfield, walked through the night, arrived at Chatsworth at 6 a.m. and immediately set the Duke's gardeners to work. Within a few years, the Duke had such confidence in Paxton that he was managing the entire estate, enhancing it with bridges and reservoirs, and having almost total control over the workforce. He also designed and built the model village of Edensor but his masterpiece was the Chatsworth Great Stove, a conservatory that was inspired by the conservatory at Syon House. Prince Albert was already familiar with the Great Stove, for he and Queen Victoria had driven to this edifice to the sound of the Royal Anthem when visiting Chatsworth in December 1843. Paxton had also secured his financial future by investing in railways.

On a visit to London, Paxton learned that the Building Committee was seeking a new design. He secured an introduction to Sir Henry Cole, inspected the Hyde Park site and proposed that an iron and glass building should be erected. This would be light and airy, cheap – partly because of the repeal of the tax on glass in 1845 – simple to erect and able to be quickly dismantled so that the iron and glass could be sold for scrap. Later Paxton said that his inspiration had been the leaf construction of the Amazonian giant water lilies he cultivated in the Great Stove, but he had benefited from experiments over many years with glass buildings. Within three days he had devised a vast prefabricated building which, on 11 June 1850, he sketched out during a meeting of the Midland Railway Company of which he was a director. Within a week detailed plans for a building 1,848ft (564m) long, 456ft (139m) wide and transepts 108ft (33m) high were presented to the committee, together with an estimated cost of £79,800, which was later raised to £85,500, submitted by Fox and Henderson, a firm of building contractors in Southwark

The committee agreed the design, providing that the building plans were altered to overarch several elm trees. This was in order to frustrate opponents who were using arguments about the destruction of the elms to cancel the whole scheme. Paxton, aided by Charles Barry, immediately sketched in an arched transept, which added impressively to the graceful aspect of the building and paradoxically appeared to lighten its bulk. In spite of more opposition, especially by *The Times* and certain Members of Parliament, building began in July 1850 and was finally completed in April 1851. Over 2,000 men worked on the site and hundreds of spectators watched in amazement at the speed with which the building was constructed. Three columns, secured by two girders, were erected within fifteen minutes. Teams of horses raised trusses to the roof. Much of the woodwork and the metal beams were prepared on site and work continued through the night, illuminated by huge bonfires fed by shavings.

Punch magazine, won over by the imaginative structure, coined the name Crystal Palace and the author W.M. Thackeray called it 'a blazing arch of lucid glass'. Opposition died away and the crisis that delayed the opening of the building was not human but avifaunal. The London sparrows delighted in the warmth and perches of what they perceived was a great aviary and the public would be spattered with their droppings. Obviously they could not be shot and poison failed. According to an apocryphal story it was the Duke of Wellington who, summoned by the Queen, had the answer: 'Try sparrowhawks, Ma'am'. The solution was completely effective.

The Crystal Palace area before 1852.

On 1 May 1851 the Queen and Prince Albert opened the Great Exhibition. The soundness of the building was evident, for a gun salute from a model frigate on the *Serpentine* failed to shatter any glass. The Commissioners and the spectators were much relieved, especially the ladies, for *The Times* had warned that shattering glass might cut them into 'mincemeat'. In her journal, the Queen described the opening with:

> the palms, flowers, statues, myriads of people filling the galleries ... the sound of the organ [with 200 instruments and 600 voices], the singing of the National Anthem and the Hallelujah Chorus ... and my dear husband, the creator of this peace festival uniting the industry and art of all nations, all this was indeed moving and as a day to live forever.

Even the Prince said that the day had been 'quite satisfactory'.

The interior housed displays and products of the wealth of the Empire and new uses to which technology might be put. The success of the Great Exhibition was assured and until October it became a magnet for over six million visitors, many meeting friends at Osler's Crystal Fountain. The exhibition made a profit of £18,000 and this, together with some of the exhibits which were temporarily stored in Gore House, was used to create the complex of museums and buildings dedicated to the arts and the sciences in South Kensington. From

being a cause of friction, the Crystal Palace had become one of London's, if not Britain's, most popular attractions. Paxton would have preferred to see his masterpiece left in Hyde Park as a 'Water Park and Garden under Glass' but was willing to accept Battersea Park and Kew Gardens as alternative sites. He wrote enthusiastically of his idea to Parliament, who postponed a decision to take down the building until 1852. There was even a proposal by Charles Burton to convert the Crystal Palace into a glass tower, 1,000ft (305m) high. In May Parliament rejected all proposals, and Fox and Henderson prepared to recoup their building costs by selling the scrap metal and glass.

top The Crystal Palace, main entrance.

above The Crystal Palace, showing the terraces and the north and south towers.

Paxton forestalled them. Not wishing to see his work destroyed, he sought a site elsewhere, finding a location, together with 200 acres of parkland, in an open area of South London. He bought land from Leo Schuster, the owner of Penge Place, formed a company to raise half a million pounds, paid Fox and Henderson £70,000, and by August 1852 the prefabricated building had been removed from Hyde Park. The grand raising of the first pillar was in the process of re-erection at Sydenham. The reconstructed building, however, had a smaller nave than that in Hyde Park – 1,608ft by 313ft (490m by 95m) – but higher, with two large wings. The roof was vaulted and the transepts were doubled in width. The height of the central transept was 168ft (51m) as opposed to 105ft (32m) in Hyde Park. Two more storeys were added, together with a basement set into the slope. The building almost doubled its volume and, although this doubled the cost, the Crystal Palace Company had no difficulty in raising the extra money. The final cost was £1.5 million for the building, two original water towers, all fittings and the layout of the park.

It had been intended to open the Crystal Palace in May 1853 but this proved optimistic. Hordes of visitors thronged the site, drawn by reports of the vast edifice. Few people had previously heard of Sydenham; now the name was recognised everywhere. Paxton was unable to prevent visits but he did ensure that no one was injured. Eventually, in 1854, it was possible to provide details for a grand opening ceremony: 500 people entertained to lunch by Fox and Henderson, a series of entertainments filling the rest of the day and in the evening the guests, replete with champagne, would wander in the gardens.

On 10 June 1854 Queen Victoria arrived with Prince Albert and members of the Royal Family to formally open the reincarnation of the Crystal Palace. Members of the House of Commons and the House of Lords, foreign ambassadors, the Lord Mayors of London, York and Dublin, and many lesser dignitaries attended. To the relief of the organisers the weather was perfect. The crowds, estimated at over 30,000, were less well behaved, as they crowded into the galleries and besieged the grounds. The next year the Queen entertained the French Emperor, Napoleon III, and the Empress Eugénie to lunch in a private room at the Palace. After the royal visitors had been taken round the Palace and the park, the Emperor was heard to remark 'What a place for a fête!'

The project enabled Paxton, newly knighted, to extend his idea of a winter palace and garden and he filled the building with rare plants and numerous casts of statuary, thus surpassing his previous work at Chatsworth. He turned the slopes of the hill into a grand park, sumptuous enough to rival any in Europe. Paxton had often visited other countries in Europe with the Duke of Devonshire and had witnessed their water displays. In addition he had designed the Emperor Fountain at Chatsworth, with its breathtaking height of 200ft (61m). The fountains at Crystal Palace would therefore rival those at Versailles. The water towers allowed Paxton to do this by producing water under pressure for the fountains. The original towers were a failure so Brunel designed towers, one at either end of the building, each 284ft (86.5m) high, with a water capacity of 300,000 gallons.

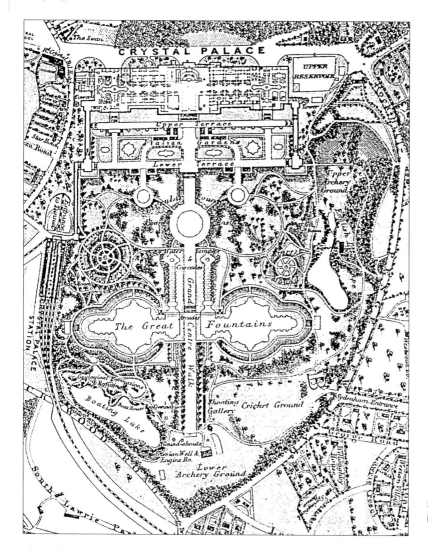

Stanford's map of the Crystal Palace and its grounds in 1862.

Brunel's water towers, which could supply 7 million gallons of water an hour, fed a system of fountains, jets and sprays situated on a series of terraces. In all over 11,000 jets of water rose high in the air. Two of 280ft (85m) rose 100ft (30.5m) higher than Nelson's Column in Trafalgar Square. Queen Victoria, Prince Albert and members of the Royal Family, who dodged the water spray blown by a disrespectful wind, attended the inauguration of the fountains on 18 June 1856. The park fountains were perhaps too ambitious. Those on the Upper Terrace were expensive to run, needing 6 million gallons for one display. They were soon abandoned. Others lacked the statuary needed to given them interest and dignity; when they were turned off, black stumps arose from blank sheets of water. The water concentrated in two huge basins, which later were filled in. The South Basin was used as a football pitch; the Cup Final was held there between 1895 and 1914. The North Basin became a cycle track. In the 1960s the site was used for the athletics track and the enclosed sports hall and swimming pool of the National Sports Centre.

There was no difficulty in filling the building with exhibits. The north nave contained a series of Fine Art Courts, designed by Digby Wyatt and Owen Jones, beginning with Byzantium and Egypt and continuing with the Medieval and Renaissance periods to the Chinese. These attempted to convey elements of art, sculpture and architecture of particular civilisations. Other areas were filled with an aquarium, a Natural History collection, an exhibition extolling the English Kings and Queens, and almost every species of stuffed animals, birds and fish. Nothing was too ambitious. People in Sydenham watched in amazement as a palm tree, 50ft (15m) tall, travelled safely to its site in a cart drawn by thirty-two horses.

The exhibits in the courts inspired painters, whose works reveal the Palace's splendid setting, the water displays and the vast expanse of its parkland. Holman Hunt stayed in Sydenham in December 1856 especially, as he wrote in a letter to Edward Lear, 'for the convenience of being near the Crystal Palace' in order to use part of the Alhambra Court for the background to his painting 'The Finding of the Saviour in the Temple', which is now in the City Museum and Art Gallery in Birmingham. Alma-Tadema incorporated motifs from the Egyptian and Classical Courts into his paintings, and Sir Edward Poynter's background to his huge 1867 canvas 'Israel in Egypt', which is in the Guildhall Art Gallery in London, owes more to the Egyptian Court at Sydenham than to any historical building in Egypt; indeed it was nicknamed 'The Egyptian Court on Canvas'.

Evening sunsets tinted over 1.5 million square feet of glass (140,000 m²) with colours of red, gold and purple, so that the glow of the building could be seen over much of south-east London. A panoramic painting of the Palace and the park by James Duffield Harding reveals the hill dominated by the Palace, the park with the fountains in full display, and the lake and islands inhabited by dinosaur models.

Aerial view of the Crystal Palace. To the left is the High Level station; to the right is the park.

These exhibits were part of the educational function of the Crystal Palace. Its main purpose, however, was to be an entertainment centre. Pride of place was given to a theatre and a concert hall, which could seat 22,000 people. Under the central transept was the Grand Orchestra and, for the next eighty years, regular performances of choral music were held with choruses of 4,000 performers and an orchestra of 440, accompanied by an organ with 4,500 pipes. If England was a music-loving nation, it liked its music joyful and loud. The first Handel Festival, held in 1859, became a regular feature with the highlight being an enthusiastic rendering of the *Hallelujah Chorus*.

To its credit the Palace had as its own musical director August Manns, a Prussian who became a naturalised Englishman. He appreciated the value of music and fought to bring the first performances of now familiar compositions to England. These included Mendelssohn's Fifth (Reformation) Symphony, Schubert's Sixth, Eighth (Unfinished) and Ninth (Great C Minor) Symphonies and Wagner's suite from *Tannhauser*. Music by English composers, such as Sterndale Bennett, Julius Benedict and Arthur Sullivan, was not neglected. The Saturday orchestral concerts drew an appreciative audience, which regularly took the trains from London Bridge or Victoria. No branch of entertainment was missed. Operettas, opera, music hall and pantomimes took place regularly. Between 1865 and 1875 an average of over 100 plays a year were performed. A Guide Book of 1888 reported approvingly: 'let us not forget that [the Crystal Palace] has fulfilled its original mission, as far as Art is concerned, in raising the standard of excellence in the performance and appreciation of high-class music'.

It was the Crystal Palace that drew many musicians and other important people to Sydenham. George Grove, the secretary of the Crystal Palace Company, and later first director of the Royal College of Music, lived first in Westwood Hill and then in a house on the site of what is now the presbytery of St Philip Neri. It was here that he compiled the first edition of *Grove's Dictionary of Music and Musicians*. Composer Arthur Sullivan often stayed with the Grove family and at one time lodged over a shop in Sydenham Road. It was from here that he conducted a doomed love affair with Rachel, one of the two daughters of John Scott Russell, the builder of the *Great Eastern* iron steamship, who lived in Westwood Lodge. Scott Russell forbade the match with what he considered a musician with no fortune and no prospects. Henry Littleton, who became the owner of the music publishers Novello & Company, entertained Anton Dvorak and Franz Liszt at Westwood House. Sir Charles Stanford stayed in Sydenham and played the organ at St Bartholomew's church.

In 1852 the directors, determined to keep Paxton close to his masterpiece, partly for prestige reasons, partly because they needed his advise, bought a house called Rockhills on a site adjoining the Palace and allowed him to live in it rent free until his death in 1865. This large, comfortable house, with its gates and posts reputed to be a gift by Queen Victoria, suited Paxton and he used it constantly, especially after he was elected as MP for Coventry and needed to be in London. He was often joined by his now companion and friend, the Duke of Devonshire, who so regarded the house as his own that he proposed numerous

below Sir George Grove.

below bottom Plaque commemorating Sir George Grove on the site of his house in Sydenham Road.

View of the interior of the Crystal Palace, showing Osler's Crystal Fountain.

alterations. Paxton's wife, Sarah, continued to live in Derbyshire and managed her husband's affairs. She constantly lamented his absence but to no avail as she knew his devotion to his work and also to the Duke. Rockhills has since been demolished and the Caravan Club now occupies the site.

In its heyday the Palace grounds were unparalleled in Britain for their variety of plants and elaborate layout. Wide steps led up to the palace, guarded by crouching sphinxes. On the lower balustrades were copies of sculptures. Terraces, intended as a formal element, were planted with floral displays. Below these, the parkland became more pastoral with walks, open areas, smooth lawns and shrubberies. At the lowest level was the boating lake with islands on which replica dinosaurs were placed. This design, apart from the dinosaur complex, followed the principles that Paxton had used in his creation of Prince's Park, Liverpool in 1842 and Birkenhead Park in 1843. In both these parks, open parkland contrasted with sections of private or formal gardens and in Prince's Park attractive walks surrounded a lake with an undulating edge. Edward Milner, who had laid out Prince's Park, was given responsibility for Crystal Palace Park and followed his mentor's beliefs.

Garden furniture included temples and statuary, a maze, grottos, lakes and islands. As the concept was presumed to be educational as well as pleasurable, the lower lake included several islands on which were placed models representing dinosaurs. The directors were pleased that Benjamin Waterhouse Hawkins, who was advised by Professor Richard Owen, created these. He had coined the name dinosaur from the Greek words for terrible lizard.

Iguanodons in Crystal Palace Park, 2004.

There were difficulties at the Crystal Palace. In June 1853 the directors received a threatening letter demanding the removal from male statues of the parts which 'in life ought to be concealed' as well as the placing of fig leaves in discreet places. If this were not done, the directors would 'see the fury of public remonstrations opening in full force against the magnificent undertaking'. The problem was solved with a hammer and chisel although there was a problem in securing the requisite number of fig leaves.

More serious was an accident that occurred in August 1853. Scaffolding in the central transept collapsed, causing the workmen to drop, as a spectator noted, 'like partridges'. Twelve men were killed and several injured. Other casualties included two horses that had been drawing carts of lime for mixing with cement up the central nave. An inquest produced a verdict of accidental death. At the funeral of ten of the men, buried in St Bartholomew's churchyard in Sydenham, at least 1,000 workmen accompanied the coffins. Many of the labourers were navvies who had worked on canals and railways, operating in self-contained groups under a leader. Some lived in a hutted area on the site; others lodged in the Sydenham, Norwood and Forest Hill areas. When the Crimean War broke out in 1854, many were recruited for an Army Work Corps. Paxton personally oversaw their recruitment, and three groups had been sent to the Crimea by 1854.

Another disaster occurred in 1861 when gales destroyed over 300ft (91m) of the north wing. This left the finances of the Palace in such a parlous state that the wing was never rebuilt. Five years later, in December 1866, the north transept containing the Alhambra, Assyrian, and Byzantine Courts, the Royal Apartments, the Library and the Indian and Naval Galleries was destroyed by fire. The north transept was not rebuilt because it was grossly underinsured. Only £200,000 was paid out when the total cost of the damage was ten times that sum.

In 2003, the Bishop of Woolwich rededicated the restored grave of workmen killed in the 1853 accident at Crystal Palace.

Initially the Palace, its exhibits and the entertainment seemed to be a resounding success. Samuel Laing, chairman of the Crystal Palace Company, had declared that if the Palace was worthy of the people of England, the people of England would flood to the Palace. He predicted over 50 million visitors a year, most of them transported by the London, Brighton and South Coast Railway. This was a decided overestimate. The reality was that an average of 2 million visitors a year, many of whom had purchased season tickets, came to be entertained and possibly educated. It became a monthly or weekly occasion to take advantage of the huge variety of shows and exhibits. Musical events were probably the most popular but there were mass meetings of societies, associations and unions under the vast Palace roof.

Pantomimes and circuses were staged. The French tightrope walker, Blondin, played musical instruments while turning somersaults, performed tricks and cooked an omelette on a stove on his high wire stretched the length of the central transept. He did not, in spite of a persistent legend, walk a tightrope between the water towers; the tension would have demolished the towers. More solemn events included a service on 7 October 1857 for the victims of the Indian Mutiny. Charles Spurgeon, one of the most eloquent and famous preachers of his day, drew a congregation of almost 24,000 people to the Central Transept to hear his sermon, which he gave without amplification, on this 'day of National Humiliation decreed for the restoration of Tranquillity in India'. A collection of over £700 was sent to the National Fund for Sufferers of the Mutiny. To the surprise of some of his listeners and the gratification of others, he connected the atrocities of the Mutiny with the toleration of prostitution in London.

Sporting events included matches of the London County Cricket Club between 1899 and 1905 with W.G. Grace as captain. Grace insisted that the Sydenham and Norwood Lawn Tennis Club, which had used tennis courts in the grounds, be given notice to quit to enable their ground to be used for the new cricket club. The manager of the Crystal Palace Company said that the Palace would be sorry to lose the tennis club but it was 'felt that alternatives would be far too public and that ladies could hardly be expected to play with pleasure'. The club found alternative premises in 1899 in Lawrie Park Road and, unlike the cricket club, is still in existence. The Crystal Palace Football Club was founded in 1871 from workmen, clerks and other officials at the Palace. The next year it reached the semi-final of the FA Cup and continued to play at the Palace until 1911. The FA Cup Final was held on the Exhibition Ground close to the Palace from 1895 until 1914; in 1913 a record 121,919 spectators watched the game. In an effort to attract new visitors, motor- and cycle racing, balloon ascents and aeronautical displays were added to the attractions.

W.G. Grace with HRH the Prince of Wales, 1910.

Spectacular shows included *Invasion*, when a village erected on a terrace in front of the Palace was attacked by a Zeppelin which dropped bombs and parachutists, the latter being overcome by gallant British troops. At least 25,000 spectators watched these evening events and double that number came for the weekly summer firework displays organised by Brock of Brock's firework company, with a grand finale of 2,000 rockets or one of Brock's set pieces. A set piece of the Battle of Trafalgar was 820ft long and displays for Queen Victoria's Jubilees included huge fiery portraits of the Queen.

Two railway stations served the Palace. The Low Level station was on the lines from London Bridge, Victoria, Croydon and Beckenham, enabling visitors to come from coast, city and suburbs. A spur line opened in 1854 from Sydenham. This was joined by a line from Wandsworth, which cut through a tunnel 2,235ft (680m) long just before the station. A covered passageway enabled visitors to walk the quarter of a mile to the Palace sheltered from inclement weather.

The London, Chatham and Dover Railway, which incorporated the Crystal Palace and South London Junction Railway in 1875, used the High Level station, opened in 1865, which was constructed by Edward Middleton Barry, younger brother of Charles Barry, in Gothic style enlivened with steep mansard roofs. Barry was previously noted for the architecture of the Royal Opera House and the Covent Garden Floral Hall. The station was a terminus, so engines were reversed on a turntable. Visitors could enter the Palace through a vaulted brick tunnel, constructed by Italian workmen and said to have been inspired by the Byzantine style. In the Second World War it served as an air-raid shelter.

Admission prices at the Palace ranged from a shilling to a guinea. Admission at half a crown usually meant a middle-class crowd arriving in first-class carriages, although there were often complaints that the railways could not supply enough suitable carriages. The Palace directors encouraged both first- and third-class visitors to come. They wanted to attract as many visitors as they could because they were becoming increasingly alarmed about the finances of the company. The enterprise had not been soundly funded from the start

Crystal Palace Parade and the High Level station.

Festival of Empire, 1911.

Aeronautical section of the Imperial War Museum in 1920. The exhibits are placed before screens depicting kings and queens.

and there were no reserve funds to bail it out. It never made the profits that the directors had predicted because of the cost of maintenance. The Crystal Palace Company went bankrupt in 1909. It was hoped that the Festival of Empire staged in 1911 would help recoup their losses. Replicas of the parliament buildings of all countries in the Dominions were built, which housed products of the respective countries. Visitors could tour the site by miniature railway and view with pride the vast extent of George V's empire. It was the last great fling. The property was sold for £250,000 to the Earl of Plymouth, who appealed for funds to save it for the nation and keep the area out of the hands of speculative builders. A Lord Mayor's Trust Fund provided the money by 1913 and things might have improved but the First World War prevented development. During the war the Palace was used by the Royal Naval Division, the Royal Naval Air Service and the Royal Naval Volunteer Reserve as HMS *Victory VI*, more popularly known as HMS *Crystal Palace*. The neglected grounds became overgrown but at the end of the war the building became the first home of the Imperial War Museum. Then the trustees had the sound judgement to appoint Henry Buckland as managing director. Accepting the post with some reluctance, he believed the Palace could be a profitable enterprise. He did not succeed, but his efforts earned him a knighthood. The building was cleaned, glass replaced and structural damage repaired. The gardens were weeded, tidied and replanted and the lake cleaned out. Visitors returned but not in great numbers. Money was tight during the Depression of the 1920s and '30s and only the firework displays drew large crowds.

On 30 November 1936 the Palace put on its final apocalyptic display, but an unintentional one. It had been a usual day. There had been a choir rehearsal, preparations for the National Cat Show had been finalised and musicians were rehearsing for a concert. At around 7 p.m. a fire swept through the central transept, down the nave and into the south-west wing. Fed by the dry exhibits, the flames burst through the roof, throwing shards of glass into the air. The Penge Fire Brigade arrived at 8.03 p.m., followed by the Beckenham Fire Brigade two minutes later. Soon fire brigades from all over London converged on the area but they were unable to put out the flames as a force 5 gale swept the flames in front of it. The fiery spectacle was visible as far as the south coast and, it was said, for fifty miles round London. Crowds filled the streets of Sydenham, Penge and Crystal Palace and on the open spaces of Blackheath and Parliament Hill in north London to watch the destruction. Startled spectators on the heights of Sydenham Hill saw not only large flights of birds rise from the aviary but also a vast, grey mass of rats leaving the burning Palace. Few saw the fish being boiled alive, although some are reputed to have survived, in the water of the central fountain.

It was said that the collapse of the Great Transept could be heard for five miles. To this day people in the area have gobbets of solidified glass as souvenirs of the greatest fire in London between the Great Fire of 1666 and that of the 1941 Blitz. By 2 a.m. only the two towers were left standing and Londoners were left to mourn a star attraction and one of their favourite places of entertainment. Not everyone grieved. In an interview for the *Daily Sketch*, George

above The Crystal Palace fire at around 8.30 p.m. on Monday 30 November 1936.

right Sir Henry Buckland standing amid the ruins of the palace on the morning after the fire.

far right The ruins of the Palace on the morning of 1 December 1936.

Bernard Shaw is reputed to have said, 'Queen Victoria is dead at last. I have no wish to see the Crystal Palace rebuilt'.

The destruction was total but incredibly the building had been insured for only £110,000, which Lloyds paid the following week. Half-hearted plans for rebuilding failed and the water towers, which had miraculously survived the fire, lasted until the Second World War when they were demolished, the reason given that they might act as guiding beacons for German bombers. After the war the area became the property of the London County Council and the Palace site was buried under 385,000 tons of rubble from bombed building sites in London. A care and maintenance programme continued until 1979 when the Crystal Palace Foundation was formed. This was a charitable volunteer organisation which planned to restore and preserve the park, in particular the stairways and balustrades. A museum was founded in the last surviving building, which, in 1872, had housed part of the Crystal Palace School of Practical Engineering. Replanting began, together with restoration of pathways.

Crystal Palace, looking north from the Lower Terrace, 2003.

In an effort to bring life to the park, the London County Council, by then the Greater London Council, encouraged the formation of a small zoo for children and erected a concrete platform as a stage for concerts. These took place on summer evenings and ended with fireworks, in a somewhat tame comparison to those that had taken place previously. In 1964 the park was divided by the building of the National Sports Centre, which cut across Paxton's central axis. Unfortunately, by the 1980s the utilitarian design was looking dilapidated.

In 1986 the Greater London Council was abolished and the Crystal Palace Park was transferred to the London Borough of Bromley. By now, much of the top site had been given to a caravan park and a television transmitter. Bromley continued to hold concerts but seemed uncertain what to do with this inheritance. Various schemes were proposed including a new leisure centre and a large hotel centred on the top site. Opposition to these schemes came to a head in 1996 when Bromley Council published proposals for a vast complex on the top site. This would include a twenty-screen multiplex cinema with a car park, restaurants, bars and what were somewhat loosely described as leisure boxes. At the same time the National Sports Centre and the park were to be refurbished. Such a scheme would generate increased traffic in the area and possibly necessitate the widening of roads. Opposition was vehement, especially when planning permission was granted in May 1999. The Crystal Palace Campaign was formed and a vigorous attack mounted, which included petitions, public meetings and eventually a legal challenge. The campaign intensified once it was known that the Sports Lottery Fund had rejected a funding bid for the National Sports Centre and the Heritage Lottery Fund had refused to fund restoration of the park except for the dinosaurs and some features of the top site. Lack of money and the level of opposition forced Bromley to give up its proposals and in 2001 the council announced that as London and Regional Properties, the proposed developers of the park, had withdrawn, they had therefore terminated any agreement with the company. It seemed unlikely that any other developer would come forward.

The Upper Terrace and the television transmitter, 2003.

The head of Paxton in Crystal Palace Park.

The campaign, however, had revealed disparate views of what the park's future might be. Ecologists wished it to be left undisturbed, especially as it comprised one of the largest open spaces in south-east London. Historians wanted the terraces to be restored, some even proposing a reconstruction of the original Crystal Palace. Those interested in recreation wanted more refreshment areas and the extension of sports facilities. A complete refurbishment of the National Sports Centre was necessary but it would be expensive to bring the facilities to Olympic standards and, the establishment of the Olympic site in the Lea Valley area meant the abandonment of these proposals. An Urban Park Forum, established in 2001, with a remit to consider public parks as a vital necessity to public recreation, was urged to include future consideration of Crystal Palace Park.

By 2004 some restoration work had been undertaken. The lake was cleared out, the dinosaurs and the geological time section were restored and new iron fencing erected. There is a passionate desire for the park to be sympathetically managed with the historic terraces restored, and the remaining sad-looking statues to be revived to their former glory, cleaned of graffiti. Other plans in 2003 had included a proposal to erect a glass building of two floors, one devoted to sculpture and the other for use as an exhibition space. Yet another plan envisaged a huge memorial, an Angel of the South, dominating the top of the hill. In 2005 the Mayor of London and the London Development Agency (LDA) took over the lease of the National Sports Centre which is now managed by Greeenwich Leisure. The running track has been relaid. In 2011 Crystal Palace Football Club announced plans to relocate the club from Selhurst Park to the site and that they would maintain the athletics track. There is still, however, the possibility that Tottenham Hotspur will continue their attempt to take on the Sports Arena. Proposals to relocate some form of motor racing in the Park also came to fruition in 2011. Maintenance of the park remains with the London Borough of Bromley but as any proposals would affect other boroughs, they keep a watching brief on these. The park is well used by the general public, especially at weekends but the huge stone head of Sir Joseph Paxton, erected in 1873, still faces away from the upper area, averting his eyes from the sad remains of his greatest achievement.

Sculpture of Pacific saved from the Crystal Palace and placed on the Dacres estate.

chapter six

Monstrous birds: Survival in two world wars

On 28 June 1914 in Sarajevo, a town barely known in Britain, Gavrilo Princip assassinated Franz Ferdinand, Archduke of Austria, and his wife Sophie. The seemingly inevitable consequence was the outbreak of the First World War. War was declared late at night on Tuesday 4 August but little had altered by the next weekend when the Crystal Palace was full of visitors enjoying the park and the exhibits. Subsequently the assassination had a dramatic effect upon the lives of the people of this London suburb.

The Aliens Restriction Act in August 1914 meant that the large number of Germans in the area had to register with the police. Many were interned and Alexandra Palace was used as a transit station. The German church closed and was not reopened until 1921. Lewisham Council opened recruiting stations and many men from the Sydenham area rushed to join up. Disillusionment with the conditions in the trenches soon set in, and casualties mounted. Towards the end of the war, however, destruction also visited the civilian population. In 1757, the poet Thomas Grey had written with prophetic foresight about a vision he could not have imagined:

> *The time will come, when thou shalt lift thine eyes*
> *To watch a long-drawn battle in the skies,*
> *While aged peasants, too amazed for words,*
> *Stare at the fleet of monstrous birds.*

Although they were not 'aged peasants', the people of Sydenham experienced a few 'monstrous birds' during the First World War; and a greater 'fleet' flew during the Second World War. The Germans had drawn up plans for bombing England as early as October 1914. They had not ratified the Land War Convention of 1907 in which Article 25 forbade the bombing of undefended places by any weapons and means whatsoever. Germany however had the means to do this, relying on her airships and Gotha planes. Airships were

Soldiers of the Army Service Corps outside the Rink cinema in Silverdale, 1916.

unreliable especially in bad weather, as had been proved by the loss of the airships L1 and L2 in September and October 1913, but Zeppelins did bomb Lewisham. Aircraft were sent over singly to try to ensure that some got through.

In September 1917 the first raids took place on Sydenham, when the German 3rd Bombing Squadron attacked. The noise of the Gothas was described as being like express trains roaring overhead. Incendiaries were dropped over a wide area from Thorpewood Avenue to Sydenham Hill and the Thorpe estate but many did not ignite. Some buildings were damaged on Sydenham Hill and in Thorpewood Avenue. Number 9 Recreation Road had its roof and an inner staircase destroyed. A more serious raid was on Whit Sunday, 20 May 1918. Thirty-four Gothas and two Gotha Giants flew over the Channel towards London. Six were destroyed as they crossed the Channel but the rest got through. A 100kg bomb dropped in Lower Sydenham damaged forty-eight houses and wrecked the fronts of houses at the junction of Fairlawn Park and Sunnydene Street. Houses at Nos 1-5 Broadway Parade in Sydenham Road, which were being used as army billets, were hit killing eighteen civilians and five soldiers and injuring twelve other people. The *Lewisham Mercury* on 24 May reported that Nos 198-202 Sydenham Road had been destroyed, including a dairy, a bakery and a marine-store dealer's shop: 'The bodies of the Delahoy family at the dairy, the dairyman, his wife and three daughters, were pulled from the wreckage, and four men who worked at J.H. Mitchell, the bakery'. A 50kg bomb dropped in Lower Sydenham failed to explode. In all, twenty-seven people were killed and were buried in Ladywell cemetery, where a memorial was erected to their memory.

Bomb damage in Sydenham Road after the air raid on 23 May 1918.

This experience was as nothing compared with the Second World War. When that war broke out in September 1939, Londoners sensed that they could be a primary target for bombing raids. The First World War had shown that planes could penetrate air defences and that precautions had to be taken. The so-called Phoney War, however, gave a breathing space and allowed the public to take precautions. Blackout regulations came into force in September and people dutifully bought black cloth from drapery stores in Sydenham and Forest Hill to make curtains, and sticky tape to criss-cross their windows to prevent the glass from shattering. The most casualties at this time, however, were reported from cycle and car accidents in the blacked-out streets. Railings surrounding parks and gardens were cut down and, in theory, were to be melted down to make war weapons. In reality, many were dumped into the sea.

The Government provided Anderson shelters and the local council arranged for their installation in gardens. Fourteen curved galvanised metal sheets bolted together to form a cover 6ft (1.8m) long and 4ft (1.2 m) wide were placed over a trench 2ft (0.6m) deep with steps at each end. Earth was plastered over the top and sandbags put in front of the entrance. Steps led down to the rudimentary shelter. These shelters gave some protection but not from a direct hit. A bomb on an Anderson shelter in September 1940 killed seven members of the Oddy family, then living in Bradford Road. Other people relied on a Morrison shelter, which was basically a rectangular steel frame with mesh sides, set up indoors. It offered some protection if the house collapsed during a raid. On the Thorpe estate, residents converted cupboards under the stairs and cellars into makeshift shelters. The general public was urged to keep sandbags and stirrup pumps available, together with buckets filled with sand or water.

People made homeless because their houses had been destroyed were to report to rest centres. Lewisham Council requisitioned empty properties to house them. These included some belonging to teachers who had had to accompany evacuated children, as several people on the Thorpe estate found when they finally returned. Assistance for the homeless and help after air raids was provided by Civil Defence who used the local cinemas for training films. The 19th London Battalion of the Home Guard operated in the Sydenham and Forest Hill areas, formed mainly from employees of the various gasworks of the South Suburban Gas Company. They worked for the company during the day and trained in the evening. The battalion took part in exercises in the area. In July 1941 it 'defended' the gasworks against 'attackers' composed of the Grenadier Guards and the Nova Scotia Regiment. These exercises were abandoned when Sydenham was bombed. The troops were ordered to rescue people from their damaged houses. The company existed until it stood down on 1 November 1944. Many employees helped with rescue work until the end of the war.

An immediate sign that the war had begun came when Food Area Officers distributed ration books before Christmas 1939. A system, based on experiences in the First World War, had been devised by 1938 and the ration books printed. When war began, Britain was far better prepared for food rationing than any other country. The key to the policy was registration. Everyone registered with a retailer, who would issue the requisite 'allowance', a word that the Government preferred to 'ration'. Retailers registered with suppliers and the linking of customer, retailer and supplier reduced the risk of fraud. Customers in Sydenham had the choice of twelve grocers ranging from chain stores such as the Home and Colonial and J. Sainsbury to independents like Arthur Hall and Frank Baker. Customers in Forest Hill had less choice. Most registered with Sainsbury's and Joseph Gosling. In Kirkdale there was the choice of Williamson's or Mrs Lubbock. Not all grocers survived the war. Victor Value in Sydenham Road and William Alder in Dartmouth Road were both destroyed in air raids. Meat was rationed not by weight, as were other food goods, but by price. Customers had the choice of ten butchers in Sydenham and three in Forest Hill. When bread rationing began in 1946, customers had the choice of registering with the chain stores or with one of the four small bakeries in Sydenham Road and the two in Forest Hill.

Another sign that the war had begun was the absence of children, for evacuation began in September 1939. Sydenham High School joined with a sister school at Brighton. A crocodile of girls marched down Westwood Hill to the station, each having a knapsack and a gas mask. Children from Sydenham County School for Girls went to Dorking. Forest Hill schools were sent to Redhill, Reigate and Oxted. Our Lady and St Philip Neri School left from Sydenham station and went to Horley. Most children drifted back by the end of the year but when the bombing began they were again evacuated to Wales and the West Country. Few, however, stayed long and by 1941 most were back in Sydenham, so the schools had to reopen. St Bartholomew's and St Michael's were among the first. They needed to reopen as newspapers reported that children were running wild in the streets, playing on bombsites and jumping on bunk beds in the shelters. Although teaching was a reserved occupation, many teachers had volunteered for the services and schools had difficulty in recruiting new ones. Later in the war, many schools sent children to harvest camps in the country during August and September to gather potatoes and to pick blackberries and rose hips to be made into vitamin drinks.

Local newspapers encouraged those who were ineligible for the forces to join the ARP service, renamed Civil Defence in 1941. One Civil Defence station, near to Forest Hill station, worked twenty-four-hour shifts. Married women often joined the Women's Voluntary Service (WVS) and engaged in canteen duties or helped with evacuation of children. The Red Cross established headquarters at Burniston in Lawrie Park Road, now St Christopher's Hospice. Nurses worked in the local hospitals but in off-duty periods or spare time made knitted goods for the services and prepared dressings and swabs. The Women's Junior Air Corps (WJAC), the Air Training Corps (ATC) and the Army Cadet Force (ACF) sought recruits. One of the best recruiting events was in September 1942 when the film *One of our Aircraft is Missing* was shown at the State cinema in Sydenham Road and 400 members of the WJAC and the ATC marched to the cinema, led by the ATC band. In November 1943 the Civil Defence, the Fire Service and the Home Guard paraded to the Capitol cinema in Forest Hill for instructional films.

The Auxiliary Fire Service (AFS) worked alongside regular firemen until both were merged into the National Fire Service (NFS) in August 1941. The main London Fire Brigade station, Station 55, was in Perry Vale. This also acted as a distribution centre for uniforms and equipment, although many firemen had to buy their own blankets and bring enough rations for their duty periods. The area was divided into five sectors, which were further divided into street fire-alarm divisions. The Sydenham sector had eight divisions, which included Newlands Park, Bell Green, Dacres Road and Bishopsthorpe Road. The Forest Hill sector also had eight divisions including Taymount Rise, Ewelme Road, Honor Oak Park and Forest Hill. The Dartmouth Road sector with its nine divisions included Dartmouth Road, Lawrie Park Gardens, Kirkdale and Sydenham Park Road. The stations' duties were divided into red, white and blue watches, forty-eight hours on duty and twenty-four hours off duty.

Accommodation had to be provided for the increased number of firemen. In September 1939 the Cedars Hotel at Cobbs Corner served as billets for the Kirkdale firemen. Some men were allocated to Wells Park Road, where an old stable had been commandeered. Station 55W took over Sydenham School in Dartmouth Road. At first they were forbidden to use the school kitchens but, later, wives and girlfriends came to cook for them. This seems to have been an enterprising station. The men supplemented their rations by buying fire-damaged goods, including tins of food that often had no labels, which turned meals into an adventurous potluck. One fireman, formerly in the Hong Kong Police, converted his colleagues to curry, which enlivened the meat ration. Another grew vegetables in the school grounds, thus dutifully obeying the Government's Dig for Victory policy.

Station 55X at Adamsrill School shared their venue with a barrage balloon unit. Barrage balloons were also stationed at Crystal Palace, Mayow Park, Alexandra Park and Wells Park, in the grounds of the Sydenham Tennis Club in

The former fire station, Station 55, in Perry Vale.

Lawrie Park Road and on other open spaces in the area. In some ways they were useless at deterring a general air attack but they did have two functions. The cables that anchored them to the ground could slice off the wing of an attacking bomber and they forced attacking aircraft to fly above them, thus reducing the accuracy of the bombing. They also acted as a deterrent to dive-bombers. One balloon tethered near to Horniman Gardens, affectionately known as Daisy, acted as a weather station and an air-raid warning: the twanging of the cable indicated the strength of the wind and the raising of the balloon meant that a raid was due. When it was moved to Kent later in the war, it was sadly missed. A few balloons had their cables cut in raids and drifted across the area, their cables banging on roofs. Searchlights stationed in several parks were operated together to form one beam of light, in the hope of trapping a German raider in it so that guns could be trained on the plane. Each park had a small barracks room for those who manned the searchlights, the balloons and the anti-aircraft guns. Many of the personnel were women who had volunteered for this duty.

During the Phoney War, when little happened but nerves were stretched, many firemen and Civil Defence workers found themselves abused by the public as people thought they were dodging service in the armed forces. Some were even attacked by irate mothers whose sons had already been conscripted. Hence public relation exercises were ordered. Station 55 held dances and social events, tickets and programmes which were printed on a small printing press in the basement of Station 55W. Firemen musicians made up a small band for dances.

This hostility changed after May 1940 when the London Blitz began. Resources were then so stretched that firemen from Station 55 had to be sent to other parts of London. On 7 September 1940, when Woolwich Arsenal and Dockyard were bombed, it was noticeable that fire engines crossing Blackheath were cheered on their way. The raids on 7 and 8 September 1940 included most of the London dockland area. Firemen from Stations 55W and 55X were sent to St Katherine's Dock, where the flames were intense. For a while they could not enter the dock, until a ship loaded with munitions was edged out into the river. Men from Station 55W were away for so long that when they got back to Dartmouth Road they found they had been officially posted as missing. Firemen recalled the hard work need to roll up the hoses stiffened with water and the agony of fingers cut by glass fragments embedded in those hoses.

On 15 August 1940 there had been a foretaste of what was to come in South London. Visitors to Crystal Palace Park on a sunny afternoon saw black clouds rise from the Croydon area as German planes bombed the Croydon aerodrome. Although it was not announced at the time, over sixty people were killed and over 280 injured, with considerable damage to the aerodrome. From then on, the wail of sirens constantly sent people to seek shelters. The blackout was strictly enforced and even torches were restricted to a slit of light. Yet people felt safe: one lady remembers being accosted by a man but was sympathetic when he said he only wanted to share her torch for part of his way home. The first air raid in Sydenham came on 25 August 1940 when the Kangley Bridge Road Industrial Estate in Lower Sydenham was bombed, destroying the Columbia Ribbon and Carbon Company factory and damaging the neighbouring Baird television factory. The workers had heeded the air-raid warning, so there were no injuries.

Sydenham also found itself in the front line in the Battle of Britain. Being so near Croydon, Kenley and Biggin Hill airfields, people could witness attacks overhead as well as seeing or hearing German planes heading for the docks, Woolwich Arsenal and central London. The intense droning of the planes making their way up the Thames on 7 and 8 September 1940 was heard in the Sydenham area and flames from the bombed districts lit up the night sky. In daytime a grey-brown smoke drifted south and ash covered part of the district. Isolated damage included a direct hit on a nursing home in Newlands Park when four people were killed. Elsewhere raids in Forest Hill flattened houses in London Road and Park Hill. In September the church and vicarage of St Michael and All Saints were destroyed; the church walls were later adapted to become a container for water storage. The church of St Philip Neri in Sydenham Road, and houses in Silverdale in Sydenham and Perry Hill in Forest Hill were destroyed. A convent in Mayow Road was hit, killing three Sisters of Mercy. The Sydenham gasworks were attacked, the first attacks of many.

Isolated bombing raids now became the norm. Sydenham and Forest Hill had no military targets but there were railway lines, which could be classified as important routes. Bombs were jettisoned as raiders made their escape. This did not make the danger any less acute; shelter had to be taken during air raids or when sirens sounded, often three or four times a day. Public shelters were built in parks, on waste ground and in the streets. The noise of bombing was accompanied by ack-ack gunfire. A battery of guns at Castlebar on Sydenham Hill rattled windows and doors when they were fired. Prime Minister Winston Churchill asserted that the noise of the guns gave people confidence that Britain was attacking the enemy, but it was impossible to judge if a 200mph plane could be destroyed at 20,000ft.

The climax of the Battle of Britain came on 15 September 1940, when British pilots counterattacked enemy planes making three daylight raids over central London. During this time, houses in Venner Road, Ewelme Road and Devonshire Road were destroyed and a nursing home in Crystal Palace Park Road received a direct hit. In all, eighteen people were killed. A Dornier bomber attacked by a RAF Spitfire crashed in the forecourt of Victoria station but one of its crew was captured after parachuting into Wells Park Road.

Bombs weighing over 4,000lbs (1,800kg), called Satan Blockbusters, caused great damage. One fell into the garden of a house on Sydenham Hill and exploded underground so that the ground heaved upwards. Unexploded bombs were a danger well after the war had ended. One was discovered in Queensthorpe Road in 1986 during the making of a garden path. By then another danger had arisen: 'Is the householder connected with the IRA?', asked the bomb disposal expert. Moonlit nights often led to heavy raids. In October 1940 a mine exploded in Bryden Grove, killing five people. December 1940 was probably the worse month. A direct hit on Joy's Cellulose factory in Dartmouth Road resulted in several firemen being taken to Lewisham Hospital for treatment for the effects of inhaling fumes. A huge fire at Cobbs Corner had to be extinguished by twenty firefighting crews. There was sometimes a shortage of firemen because they had to be sent to other parts of the country. Firemen from Station 55 were sent to Birmingham for a while.

Bomb damage to Nos 23-29 Longton Grove, 1941. (Courtesy of the Imperial War Museum)

Bomb damage at Cobbs
Corner, 1940. The safe had
fallen from the top floor but
still remained intact with the
ledgers safe inside.
(Courtesy of the Imperial War
Museum)

But it was not only south-east London that suffered. On 29 December 1940 a force of 120 bombers attacked the City of London; blood-red flames illuminated the night sky as the City and the East End burned. It was reminiscent of John Evelyn's comment on the Great Fire of 1666: 'All the skies were of a fiery aspect, like the top of a burning oven; and the light seen above forty miles round about'. From the top of the Crystal Palace hill, watchers thought that the whole of London was on fire. It was said that the Crystal Palace water towers acted as guides for German bombers and so the south water tower was taken down in 1940 and the north tower in 1941.

Through all this there was a grim stoicism. The Mass Observation organisation reported that people were fed up, not only with the constant bombing and having to seek shelter, but also with the privation of rationing and the problems of getting to work. During raids people stuffed cotton wool into their ears to cut out the noise; many became temporarily or even permanently deaf. When a bomb exploded, nearby houses shook; shrapnel rattled on roofs and fell into

Controlled demolition of the North Tower, Crystal Palace in April 1941.

The last remaining fire hydrant in Sydenham, in Queensthorpe Road.

gardens and streets. Schools and church halls became rest- or rehousing centres for those who had been bombed out, although many made their own arrangements to stay with relatives or friends. Some people had to move several times. A couple living in Tannsfeld Road moved to Newlands Park when a bomb landed in their garden. They had to move on when an unexploded shell crashed though the roof of that house. When they moved back to their own house, they discovered that, although neighbouring houses had been damaged, their own was almost unscathed.

When a house was bombed, repair workers were sent out by the local council to patch up the damage. A resident in the next borough remembers a lorry coming round loaded with roof tiles, offering them to anyone who needed them. Householders took on workmen seeking employment, to repair any damage. Not everyone was protective of damaged property. Some people returned to their damaged houses to find other people rummaging through them to find replacement goods for their own losses so the first essential was to make a damaged house as secure as possible. Appeals were made for clothing, furniture and domestic equipment to be distributed to the homeless. The WVS organised both clothing stores and emergency feeding centres. Many services were controlled by London County Council or Lewisham Borough Council. Gas, electric and water companies did their best to ensure supplies, although often a pipe had to be cut off to prevent further damage. When water pipes were destroyed, rats were seen moving into houses and shelters. Damage to a house often occurred a long time after the war had ended. To this day ceilings may develop cracks or even fall because of the shaking they received in the war. At one time, it was not unusual to come downstairs in the morning and find a ceiling on the floor.

The police were worried about people standing in the street to watch planes passing overhead. A former pupil at Sydenham High School recalls ignoring gunfire when chatting to friends and being ordered to shelter by her anxious French teacher: 'Girls, girls, go inside at once. Don't you hear the bombs?' Commuters on the East Croydon to London Bridge line often found a notice in the morning saying that the line was blocked because of bomb damage or an unexploded bomb on the track. They then tried to make their way into London by hitching a lift on a lorry or waiting for a bus, for the buses took a pride in trying to run to schedule. Although people showed determination in getting to work despite the effects of the bombing, for many it was because they had to work as they needed the money. On the whole people tried to live normal lives, help their neighbours and generally soldier on.

Volunteer fire patrols, many manned by Boy Scouts, were organised to report incidents and to put out minor fires. Cinemas which had closed at the beginning of the war reopened to provide entertainment. The Government had ordered that Double Summer Time should be observed, which meant that from June into August it did not get dark until nearly midnight. This was intended to help agricultural workers but it also allowed Londoners to get home in the light, have a meal and then go out for Civil Defence or firefighting duties before dark. In addition, it meant that night-time raids occurred later.

Sydenham gained its own Victoria Cross holder in November 1941. Captain Philip Gardner of Oaklands in Silverdale, who had been awarded the Military Cross in June 1941, was awarded the VC while serving with the Royal Tank Regiment at Tobruk. He took two tanks to the rescue of two armoured cars of the King's Dragoon Guards, which were under heavy attack. While one of the tanks gave covering fire, Gardner hitched a towrope to one of the cars, and then lifted into it a wounded officer. The towrope broke, so Gardner returned to the armoured car, but was immediately wounded. In spite of this he transferred the wounded man into the second tank and returned him to the British lines. The citation commented that he did this with 'courage, determination and complete disregard for his own safety'. Later he was taken prisoner and, at the end of the war, was released by the Americans who had captured the POW camp near Brunswick.

During 1941 the destruction included Ghinn's Drapery Store in London Road, the Forester's Arms in Perry Vale and part of the Honor Oak Park estate, where thirty-one people were killed in a direct hit on Hilton House. Danger also came from parachute mines, or landmines as they were generally called. This was a form of magnetic mine about 9ft (2.7m) long and 2ft (0.6m) in diameter, containing up to a ton of explosive, which fell silently, dangling from the end of a greenish parachute. At least thirty of these fell in south-east London, causing immense damage. One in Elsinore Road damaged or destroyed 144 houses, killed two people and injured 144. Landmines fell in Silverdale, Mayow Road and Perry Vale, where fifty houses were demolished. The Sydenham gasworks received a direct hit on one of the gasometers. On one moonlit night, two landmines could be seen descending on Dartmouth Road, Sydenham and Devonshire Road, Forest Hill. The resulting explosion in Dartmouth Road destroyed shops and houses, damaged Sydenham police station and Sydenham County School and killed twenty-one people. One man always remembered having to look after the bodies until they were removed to a mortuary. Firemen from Station 55W based at the school had already been called out to incidents in central London and it was left to the police station to deal with the devastation, although six policemen were among the casualties.

There was a lull until January 1943, when an unexpected raid destroyed Sandhurst Road School in Catford, where thirty-eight children and six teachers were killed. In the same air raid, barrage balloons were destroyed at Horniman Gardens and Lawrie Park Road. Planes also strafed Tyson Road with machine-gun fire and set alight another gasometer at Bell Green. Three children who were walking home to lunch had a narrow escape: two of them ran down the side of the house and crouched against the wall until the plane had gone and as the third child ran into the house, bullets hit the door. In October 1943, houses were destroyed in Derby Road, Forest Hill, killing two people, and Earlsthorpe Road, Sydenham, where four people were killed. A boy from Essex, who was visiting his relations, was injured. This bomb also destroyed shops in Sydenham Road, including the Victor Value grocers, Dewhurst butchers, Miss Tatham's café, Miss Fowle's drapery shop and John Bowler's greengrocers. In the State cinema on the opposite side of Sydenham Road, 300 patrons escaped injury as the building survived the shock waves. After the war, the shops and houses were rebuilt. The different architecture is clearly visible in Sydenham Road but the rebuilt houses in Earlsthorpe Road are similar to those of neighbouring ones.

Sydenham Road in 2003, showing part of the Grand Parade rebuilt after the bomb destruction of 1943.

Incendiary bombs also fell in the area. In January 1944 they caused numerous fires in the Sydenham area. It was the turn of Forest Hill in March, when over seventy serious fires were started, especially in Perry Rise, Perry Vale and Vancouver Road. It was not only bombs that caused damage. Shells fired by defending guns crashed back to earth, destroying houses in Stanstead Road and Devonshire Road where the Lloyd family could not find protection under their Morrison shelter.

In 1944 the bombing entered a new phase when the area became a target for V1 flying bombs, nicknamed Doodlebugs. These, launched from sites in the Pas de Calais, had a flight time of twenty minutes to London with a speed of 350mph. These were more psychologically unnerving than conventional bombs as their flight path was unpredictable. As the two-stroke engine cut out, the V1 glided towards the ground, exploding on contact. It was the silence that caused people to take shelter or throw themselves on the ground. The British Government deliberately gave false information about where they landed so that the Germans would reduce the range of the bombs, thus causing them to crash away from central London, even if they fell on south London. The only defence against them were the RAF fighters and the barrage balloons. However, many of the latter had been moved from south-east London to the South Downs in the hope that they would intercept bombers there. On a clear day, this floating array of huge, silvery elephants were clearly seen from the higher parts of Sydenham and Forest Hill.

Inspecting a bombed site in Stanstead Road, Forest Hill.

RAF balloon barrage defence against the flying bombs. (Courtesy of the Imperial War Museum)

In June 1944 V1s fell in the Forest Hill area. The most severe incident was on 23 June, when V1s fell constantly over south-east London. One V1 hit the station then fell directly on the pedestrian subway, killing three people and injuring eighteen. It demolished a factory in Hindsley Place and damaged buildings in London Road and Devonshire Road. The railway line from London was blocked. Yet nothing in the Sydenham and Forest Hill area could equal the destruction and loss of life caused by the V1 which hit the central shopping area in Lewisham High Street in July 1944. Fifty-one people were killed and 311 injured. Throughout July and August, V1s continued to fall on Sydenham and Forest Hill, destroying houses over a wide area. In September, however, it seemed that the danger was over because the Canadian Army captured the launching pads in the Pas de Calais.

On 7 September 1944 the Home Secretary, Herbert Morrison, announced that the battle for London had been won, only to be spectacularly contradicted when, the next day, a more powerful V2 rocket with a range of 220 miles and a speed ten times that of the V1 fell on London. The V2 was fired from sites in Holland, its flight time to London was five minutes and the fuse could activate 10ft (3m) from the ground. Again the Government issued false information as to where the rockets fell so that the Germans would believe they were overshooting London and shorten the range. The Government also remained silent as to the loss of life and destruction, which meant that the general public had no idea what the south of London was undergoing. Sydenham and Forest Hill suffered attacks from V2s between November 1944 and March 1945.

On 3 November 1944 a V2 burst in the air over Sydenham High School in Westwood Hill. An eyewitness reported an enormous bang, which caused one class of children to look up from their work. The teacher calmly told them to continue with their algebra. Within a few minutes, a child who was looking out of the window reported that huge pieces of metal were falling into the grounds in front of the school. Other children told their teachers that pieces were falling into the hockey field behind the school. The headmistress, Miss Yardley, came round to each class and told the children that no one was to go outside or leave the school until the police gave them permission. The police and air-raid wardens were seen searching the grounds to collect every piece of metal, so that they could be pieced together to add to the knowledge of the mechanism of the V2. On that occasion, there was no loss of life but two weeks later a rocket fell on Kilgour Road in Forest Hill destroying seven houses, killing eleven people and injuring twenty-three. In January 1945 another V2 fell in the grounds of Sydenham County School and in March one hit a Victorian house in Crystal Palace Park Road which had been converted into flats. This house was not rebuilt and a grassed plot now marks the entrance to Crystal Palace Park. In the same month, a V2 fell in Panmure Road killing fourteen people and injuring eighty. The rocket had fallen into gardens but the blast caused over ten houses to cave in from the rear. The final rocket fell on Orpington in March 1945 and with it the destruction in London ceased.

On 8 May 1945 Germany surrendered. Even on that day the local paper reported that there were long queues of people waiting for their weekly rations. Some people celebrated in pubs, although the Forester's Arms in Perry Vale carried the sad notice: 'We have been Bombed, Blasted and Burnt. But have always opened. Today, VE Day, we are closed. No supplies. We are sorry'. Other pubs were luckier and had enough beer for celebrations. Lewisham Council held a thanksgiving parade, but asked people to defer their celebrations until the week of 3 June, which was to be designated as an official celebrations week with a march past the Mayor of Lewisham and a thanksgiving service. Sydenham could not wait so long and there were street parties in many streets including Kangley Bridge Road, Kelvin Grove and Prospect Road. Highclere Street pooled its rations to hold its party, with buns and cakes for thirty-seven children; the rations included fourteen pints of milk, five pounds of sugar and two pounds of tea. Rowland Grove was reported to have had so much food left over that the remainder was sent to the Sydenham Children's Hospital. A party in Venner Road included a treasure hunt, races and a tea. Dancing, 'accompanied on a gramophone', lasted until midnight

Silverdale held a party for children and 'shelter tenants'. The latter were those who had made most use of the shelters and the local paper noted that these included Mrs O'Neil, 'Sydenham's most bombed woman'. Larkbere Road and Wells Park Road lit huge bonfires. Some people mistakenly burned their ration books but rationing was to continue until 1954 and the local papers soon had full-page advertisements headed 'How to get your new Ration Book'. Other people stayed in central London or made their way there.

One Sydenham eyewitness reported that she joined others during the afternoon in St James's Park, which was full of people just sitting quietly in apparent disbelief that the war, at least for Europe, was over. Other people joined in the evening celebrations around Whitehall and the Mall. When the war finally ended in August 1945, VJ Day was celebrated in a more muted fashion as if everyone had already expended his or her energies. The local papers did not seem to want to spend their meagre paper ration on information about the occasion.

In July 1939 Winston Churchill had described London as the greatest target in the world, 'a kind of tremendous, fat, valuable one, ready to attack by beasts of prey'. He was concerned that when the attacks happened people would flee to the countryside, causing great transport problems. This did not happen. People in Sydenham and Forest Hill seemed to have stayed put. The public listened to announcements, partly with cynicism, partly with fatalism but were mainly concerned with getting to and from work, going about their defence duties and generally living as normal a life as possible. The first raid on Lewisham had occurred on 17 April 1940 and the last on 11 March 1945. There had been innumerable air attacks and 402 flying-bomb attacks in the south London area. In Lewisham there had been over 1,700 fatalities and over 2,000 injured. At least 200 people had been killed and over 450 injured in 120 incidents in the Sydenham and Forest Hill areas. This is probably an underestimate. Thousands of houses had been damaged, many so badly that they had to be demolished. Repairs and rebuilding of houses took place slowly in the 1950s, partly because of the lack of building materials. Many were rebuilt without the detail that had enhanced pre-war houses. An example of this can be seen at the flats on London Road in Forest Hill, where the rebuilt parts show this lack of detail.

Church buildings suffered severely in the war. Two that survived intact were St Bartholomew's church and Christ Church in Forest Hill. St Matthew's church in Panmure Road and St Michael's and All Angels were both destroyed. St Matthew's was abandoned but a new St Michael's was built in 1958. Our Lady and St Philip Neri was one of the first churches to be destroyed in 1940. A new church was opened in 1959. Both St Philip the Apostle and Holy Trinity were badly damaged. The former was replaced by a low building, although the school remained intact and was later occupied by the Seventh Day Adventists. The latter was repaired but found to be on uncertain foundations and so was demolished in 1981. St Paul's church in Waldenshaw Road, Forest Hill was destroyed. After the war, this church was linked with St Paul's in Taymount Rise, where damage had been repaired, only for that church to suffer a decline in the congregation and to be converted into flats in 1996. The Wesleyan Methodist church in Dartmouth Road was abandoned, used as a store and demolished in the 1950s. The German Evangelical church, which was destroyed in December 1940, was rebuilt as the Dietrich Bonhoeffer church in 1959. Bonhoeffer had been pastor at this church between 1933 and 1935, when he returned to Germany to oppose the Nazi party. With its impressive archive, it is one of the most important churches in south London. Some churches that were hardly damaged suffered a decline in their congregations and were demolished, for example St John's Presbyterian church in Forest Hill, which was demolished in 1983. Although no important public buildings were lost, if the destruction of churches, streets and large houses is taken into account, it is clear that the war resulted in a change in the landscape.

ST. MICHAEL'S CHURCH.   LOWER SYDENHAM.

left St Michael and All Angels' church, destroyed in 1940.

below left Dietrich Bonhoeffer church in Dacres Road, built to replace the German Evangelical church, which was destroyed in 1940.

below right War memorial to the employees of the South Suburban gas board at Livesey Hall, Lower Sydenham.

chapter seven

Twentieth-century change

In January 1901 Queen Victoria died. It seemed the end of an era, although the First World War perhaps better marks the discontinuity. There was an outpouring of mourning. The local draper's shops, Cobb's and Mayo's, following the trend in central London, organised window displays of funereal black garments; the smaller stores, such as Wellsted's and Ellis's in Sydenham Road, Jamison's in London Road, and Mann's and Osborne's in Perry Vale, followed suit. Horses with black plumes drew the horse buses, which plied between Sydenham and Forest Hill.

The new century was marked in Forest Hill by the opening of the Horniman Museum, a result of the beneficence of Frederick Horniman. The Horniman family had made its fortune in the tea trade, first in China tea then in Indian tea. John Horniman, Frederick's father, had started a tea business in 1826. Tea, by then, had become the cheap drink of the working classes and was particularly welcomed because it was made with boiling water, thus killing bacteria. Much of the tea sold was, however, adulterated with dust, dried leaves, used tea leaves and even sawdust. It was not until the passing of the Food and Drugs Act in 1875 that such practices could be prevented. Horniman had anticipated this act by inventing a machine that wrapped up the tea in sealed packets, ensuring both the purity of the tea and a growth in sales.

Frederick joined the family business but he was passionately interested in ethnography and collected from dealers and missionaries. Later he travelled widely, especially in the Far East. According to the 1901 Museum Report, he became an avid collector 'of objects likely to interest and inform those whom circumstances prevent from visiting distant lands'. He had moved from Coombe Cliff in Croydon in 1860 and lived in Surrey House on London Road, Forest Hill. His house gradually filled with his collection and was opened to visitors by appointment on two afternoons a week. By 1890, it was opened on three days a week and the number of visitors rose steadily. Eventually Horniman, under pressure it is said from his wife, moved to Surrey Mount, another house in the fifteen-acre grounds, leaving Surrey House to the collection.

The collection soon outgrew this house. In 1898 the house was demolished, and in 1901 the Duke of Fife opened a purpose-built museum, designed by Harrison Townsend. This, according to Pevsner, was 'one of the most original Art Nouveau buildings anywhere in England'. The mosaic design on the front, 'Humanity in the House of Circumstance', added to its charm. Horniman insisted that the museum and the grounds should be open to the public in perpetuity for their 'recreation, instruction and enjoyment', thus echoing the ideals of the directors of the Crystal Palace. The number of visitors steadily increased, helped by a tram service from Forest Hill to Camberwell, which conveniently stopped outside the museum, and the proximity of the nearby Forest Hill railway station.

School visits were popular, so an educational programme was begun in 1902 with Saturday morning lectures for teachers. By 1906 lectures were being held on Saturday afternoon for the general public and, six years later, a lecture hall and a library were added. The Horniman Museum soon became one of the most popular museums in London, especially as the gardens provided recreational space. A bandstand was added to the grounds in 1906, and a toy boating lake was another attraction. As the collection grew so the museum expanded. Another hall was added in 1933 and an education centre in 1967. In 1995 a Centre for Educational Understanding (CUE) was added, utilising the best feature of environmental architecture with pine walls and a living roof of grass and wild flowers. To commemorate the museum's centenary a programme of extensive rebuilding was undertaken.

Frederick Horniman and his staff at the Horniman Museum.

Ethnological Saloon at the original Horniman Museum, 1891. Frederick Horniman stands second from the left.

As well as the Horniman Museum, Forest Hill had another recreational venue which became popular during the early twentieth century. This was the public baths, opened in 1885 by the Earl of Dartmouth, who hoped that the baths might bring health and comfort to the working classes. There were two large swimming pools, tiled in the traditional Victorian manner with white glazed brick. With due propriety, ladies were to have the use of the first-class baths exclusively on two afternoons a week. The first-class baths cost 6d and the second-class baths 2d per session. In addition, there were private or slipper baths with separate entrances for men and women. These baths were especially valuable in an age when few houses had a bathroom. Lewisham provided a public bathhouse in 1907 at Bell Green to serve Lower Sydenham. The slipper baths became a popular meeting place for women, where gossip and social chat could be exchanged. Still in use until after the Second World War, they provided an amenity for people who were bombed out or awaiting housing refurbishment. During the interwar years, the main pools were often boarded over to provide areas for concerts, dances and sports activities. The pools were refurbished in the 1920s and their tiling upgraded. In 1996 Lewisham Borough Council decided to close the Forest Hill baths because of the cost of maintenance, stating that the swimming pools at the National Sports Centre, Crystal Palace, and the BP Sports Centre at Lower Sydenham were adequate. A campaign was immediately started to save the pools, especially as they provided basic swimming facilities for schools and clubs. The campaign succeeded and the pools are still a popular attraction.

Forest Hill Swimming Pools

Wells Park, 1908.

More recreation space was provided with the opening of Wells Park in 1901. The area had been fields, a surviving part of Westwood Common. London County Council laid out eighteen acres, making use of ponds, possibly from the same source as the original well water. In the same year the environment in Lower Sydenham was enhanced when Home Park was created out of the grounds of Home Park Lodge.

The children's hospital in Lower Sydenham also provided for the health of the community, although its fame soon spread beyond Sydenham. Additional beds had been provided and in 1923 the outpatients' department was rebuilt. Three years later Queen Mary opened a nurses' home. Royal favour guaranteed general approval so the name was changed to the South Eastern Hospital for Children. The Duchess of Kent opened a new wing in 1935 and the extra space proved invaluable during the Second World War, when adults and children were treated after bombing raids. After the war there was further reorganisation so that the hospital had five wards as well as an outpatients' department and specialised units. By the 1980s, however, facilities were merging with a

Louise House, the former
Girls' Industrial Home.

Sydenham Library. In 1962
the central porch and steps
were replaced by a window.

purpose-built specialist children's unit in Lewisham Hospital. The children's
hospital was closed, and in 1991 it was demolished and flats built on the site.

If cleanliness and cultural activities had progressed, so had educational facilities. Forest Hill opened its library in 1900 in a striking Arts and Craft building.
When the position of chief librarian was advertised, seventy-seven applications
were received. Sydenham Library opened in 1904, paid for by the steel mag-
nate and benefactor Andrew Carnegie. Both buildings were large and airy, with
ample space for books and readers.

In 1903 London County Council replaced the London School Board and took
over the part of Sydenham Hill School housed in the Sydenham Lecture Hall to
create the Sydenham Technical Institute. In the 1950s it became the Shackleton
School for Girls and is now is the Kirkdale Learning Centre. Sydenham Hill
School became the Forest Hill Central School for Boys in 1927 and ten years
later became Kelvin Grove Elementary School. It was from these two schools
that most of the evacuation of children was organised in 1939 and 1940.

In 1934 Sydenham High School moved to better premises across Westwood Hill. The main block was in Horner Grange, a large house built in 1882 which was later used as the Twilight Nursing Home and as a hotel. This provided more accommodation for the pupils; the ballroom became a dining room and gymnasium, and the school was able to use the large grounds as a sports ground. More buildings were added but the original building remained the heart of the school until fire destroyed a large part of the old house in 1997. This building has now been restored to its former splendour with suitable additional accommodation for the school.

Sydenham School was founded in Westbourne Drive in the 1860s, as a private school. It moved to Manor Mount in 1887 and was taken over by London County Council as a girls' school in 1905. In 1917 it moved to its present site, where it was housed in a pleasant red brick building, and was refounded as a girls grammar school. After the war it became a comprehensive school, amalgamating with Shackleton School. A large teaching block was added, designed by Basil Spence, and in 1973 a further block was added for Sixth Form studies. After the war, in 1956, Forest Hill Boys' School, a comprehensive school, was built on land cleared to create the Dacres estate. Later it added an arts block and a sports hall.

Primary schools were repaired and rebuilt after the war. St Michael's in Champion Crescent built a new hall on the site of the former church. St Bartholomew's closed the old school on Kirkdale in 1973 and built a new school. Holy Trinity School, established in Dartmouth Road in 1872, recently undertook substantial rebuilding and refurbishment. New schools

Entrance hall of Sydenham High School.

Sydenham County School staff, 1937.

The Basil Spence building,
Sydenham School.

Queen's Hall cinema,
Sydenham Road, c. 1918.
It was demolished in 1943
after bomb damage.

were built: Eliot Bank School and Horniman School. The latter, built in 1972, commands a steep hillside site in Horniman Drive. Kelvin Grove has added an attractive infant school. The old Kelvin Grove School is still housed in the former London Board school building, as is Haseltine School in Lower Sydenham. Our Lady and St Philip Neri renovated its old school, which was built in 1874.

Between 1910 and 1967 cinemas were major sources of entertainment. The Rink opened in Silverdale in 1909 for roller skating, billiards and refreshments, and switched to showing films the next year. During the First World War the army commandeered it but held concerts there for the public. The cinema closed in 1940 and became an ARP post. The Sydenham Picture Palace opened in Sydenham High Street in December 1910 but lasted only a year. The building is now No. 163 Kirkdale. The Queen's Hall cinema in Empire Parade, Sydenham Road opened in the same year and had a longer existence. It was a classical style building with a central arch supported by two columns. It was commandeered by the army from 1917 to 1919 but then resumed showing films until it was demolished after being bombed in the Second World War. All three cinemas were small in comparison with the State cinema, built on the corner of Girton Road and Sydenham Road, which seated 954 people. It opened in 1931 and was the most popular source of entertainment in the area. It became the Gaumont in 1949. In 1969 the proprietors sought to replace it with a supermarket. They bought two houses in Girton Road and demolished them to form a rear access. They succeeded in 1971, and a supermarket now stands on the site.

Forest Hill also had three cinemas. The Picture Playhouse, opened in 1910, was housed in a converted shop in Dartmouth Road and seated about 450. Although it was refurbished and renamed the Empire in 1912, it was never successful and closed during the First World War. The Stanstead Picture Palace in Wastdale Road was created in a vacant shop in 1913. For publicity the manager invited 600 Scouts to attend one of the first shows. In 1918 Albert Goosens was employed, at the start of what was to be a distinguished musical career, to lead a small orchestra playing light and classical music. In 1931 it was renamed the Astoria, only to become the Balmoral in 1954, then the New Astoria the following year. It became a Bingo Hall in 1965. By 1975 it was derelict and so demolished. The longest-lasting cinema was the Capitol in London Road. This opened in 1929, flourished until 1966 and survived a plan to alter its façade. It was given Grade II listed status, which helped to preserve it for use after 1966 as a bingo hall. It was transformed into a public house in 1997.

There had been a pause in the growth of the area after 1870 but this was only temporary. Small houses in undistinguished terraces gradually covered the open space between Stanstead Road and Forest Hill. A prominent local builder, Edward Christmas, displayed his idiosyncrasies in a group of houses which he built in Perry Vale. He gave to one group of houses names beginning with the initial letters of his wife Laura and daughter Grace. The Christmas name was, so he thought, fixed in perpetuity in the initial letters of the names he gave to Nos 108-116 Perry Vale. Christmas also built houses in Thorpewood Avenue and Radlett Avenue.

Further south, villas were built between Perry Vale and Mayow Road from 1900. There was no attempt at great differentiation and terraces of similarly

Interior of the Capitol public house in Forest Hill, 2003.

above Doorway of Hildaville, the 'H' of the Christmas houses.

opposite Map of 1894 showing the extent of land belonging to the Mayow Adams family before 1900. At one time their land stretched to Perry Vale.

designed houses with small front and rear gardens were normal. An attempt at a more interesting style of architecture came when Edmundson & Sons built the Thorpe estate. The Mayow Adams family, which had held land in Sydenham since the eighteenth century, had begun to relinquish this. They had already developed Dacres, Inglemere and Mayow Roads, but the Old House in Sydenham Road, with its extensive grounds, blocked development. After Mayow Wynell Adams' death in 1898, the Old House was demolished and large houses with decent-sized gardens were built in what became Bishopsthorpe and Queensthorpe Roads. Building continued on other roads until the 1920s and, in spite of the damage sustained in the Second World War, the Thorpe estate remains intact. It has recently been designated a conservation area.

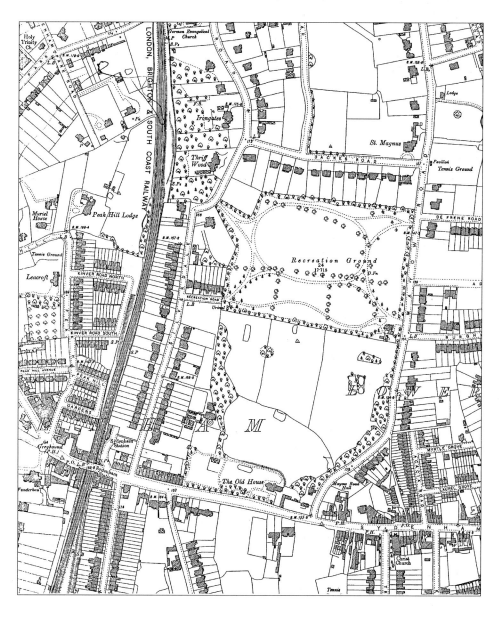

The removal of the Old House also altered the shopping pattern in Sydenham, because the Grand Parade of shops with flats above was begun in 1900 on what had been the gardens of the Old House. This, with the extension of Walter Cobb's premises in 1902, gave a new impetus to the area. The main shopping centre had previously been in Sydenham High Street, which is now Kirkdale and part of Dartmouth Road. The shopping centre moved to Sydenham Road, although many small shops continued to trade in the former area.

Forest Hill also changed. The opening of the Horniman Museum stimulated building and houses began to fill the area behind the museum after 1910, although some land, for example in Ewelme Road, was not used until the 1930s. Many of these houses had an extended view over London or towards Kent so they were in great demand. A group of houses to the west of what was later the Sainsbury's site was built in 1904. But the largest development was on London Road: King's Garth and Prince's Garth had been built, under other names, in 1850 and in 1906 Arthur Dorrell extended these and converted them into flats, seemingly without any reference to London County Council, which was then faced with a *fait accompli*. A community spirit evolved which resulted in the formation of a tennis and croquet club in 1906. The flats had long gardens behind which remained inviolate until they were sold for housing development in the 1950s.

London Road in Forest Hill was becoming a useful shopping centre but in doing so it took custom from Dartmouth Road. The west side of that road was still blocked by Newfield House and Lansdowne House and their gardens. Edward Christmas, whose business had been founded in 1888, and who, according to his advertisement, had for 'years been proving its claim to public confidence', demolished his building premises in around 1900, replacing them with small shops. The most important shops in Forest Hill were Cullen's grocery

The Old House was the home of the Mayow Adams family who owned the largest estate in Sydenham. It was demolished in 1901.

top Queensthorpe Road, 1907.

above Queensthorpe Road, 2004.

store, on the corner of Devonshire and London Roads, J.E. Barton's 'Cash Draper and Costumier', and C.F. Mayo's drapery store. Cullen's was demolished in 1915 when the road was widened. In spite of Barton's being 'large and roomy, conveniently arranged in every respect and furnished with a staff of assistants who all appear well up to their business', the business declined. Mayo, who had bought shops on either side of his own, prospered until 1930 when the Depression forced him to close.

Sydenham Road, 1904.

Sydenham Road, 2004.

Kirkdale, Sydenham.

Kirkdale, formerly Sydenham
High Street, 1907.

Before 1919 housing in Forest Hill and Sydenham had been left to private builders. In 1918 Lloyd George's government had won an election on the 'Homes for heroes' policy, whereby local councils would provide houses for returning soldiers. Such council housing, in most parts of Britain, took the form of semi-detached houses with small gardens. Lewisham Council followed this pattern in other parts of the borough but in Sydenham the only council development was Kent House Buildings in Bell Green, where five blocks of flats with little architectural merit were built. Perversely these survived the Second World War. A block of private flats was built in Kirkdale in 1934. Small private houses were also built close to the industrial estates at Kangley Bridge Road and Worsley Bridge Road. In Forest Hill two kinds of housing were built. 'Luxury flats on the West End model' were constructed and numerous houses were turned into bedsits for single or young married people who worked in the City. Southern Railway advertised itself as having a very splendid service of electric trains 'which enable the journey to be made in speed and comfort'.

Apart from this there was little building. The destruction of the Crystal Palace in 1936 decreased interest in the area. The fact that Sydenham and Forest Hill were south of the river and not connected to London by the Underground also contributed to their relative unpopularity. The destruction of houses in the Second World War disrupted settled communities. During the war almost 3,000 houses had been requisitioned and Lewisham Council was reluctant to restore them to their original owners, who tearfully pleaded with the council for their return. One determined lady sat in the council offices daily from the time they opened until the time they closed for over a month before she finally regained her house. Many houses had been divided into flats or housed several families. In some areas the situation was said to resemble Russia after the Revolution.

Both the Labour and Conservative parties favoured building flats because they felt these would house more people in a limited space. Tower blocks won approval as being the answer to the housing crisis. Sydenham and Forest Hill were ripe for development because demolition of large houses with extensive grounds would provide ample building space. Between 1948 and 1949 Byron Close, overlooking Home Park; Sunderland Mount in Sunderland Road; and Shackleton Close, off Thorpewood Avenue, were built. London County Council compulsorily purchased St Mary's House in Sydenham Hill, a retreat administered by Brompton Oratory, and forestalled Lewisham Council in providing more building in this area by consructing 400 flats on the site. The Corporation of London followed by building the Lammas Green estate in 1957. Lewisham Council looked with covetous eyes on the Dulwich side of Sydenham Hill but the Dulwich College estate had its own plans for developing the area. Lewisham had to be content with securing Round Hill House to build a small estate there.

In 1965 Lewisham and Deptford Councils united to form the London Borough of Lewisham, which gave the council a nearly permanent Labour majority. More development quickly followed. The Forest Hill estate had four large tower blocks on the sloping area facing London Road; two tower blocks were built on the hill near Eliot Bank. In 1967 the Hillcrest estate was built below the ridge of Sydenham Hill, on a site that included the former High Level railway. This part of Sydenham and Forest Hill, which had been comparatively free from housing, became a densely populated area. A huge clearance of houses took place in the Wells Park area. As early as 1912 Walter Besant had referred to this area as an embryo slum and during the Second World War it had suffered severely from both bomb and rocket attacks. Nevertheless the area had revived with a strong community spirit and its wide variety of shops attracted customers. However, this did not prevent whole streets, such as Bradford Road, being swept away in spite of intensive lobbying. The sense of community spirit was dissipated when people from Deptford were moved into blocks of flats. The one survivor was Halifax Street, originally Hanover Street, which had been built in the 1840s. It later became a conservation area and is a model of what could have been achieved.

Tower blocks overlooking Home Park replaced a council depot. Others were built north of Mayow Park to form the Dacres estate, and Silverdale lost many of its individual houses in the 1960s and 1970s. Further replacement of houses by tower blocks recalled Pevsner's remark that 'public housing is plentiful but mostly unmemorable'. This onslaught led to the foundation of the Sydenham Society in 1972, which produced a handbill headed 'Save our Sydenham'. It drew attention to the ever-expanding intentions of the council and warned in capital letters, 'Your road could be the next to be threatened by Lewisham Council'. The Sydenham Society failed to stop the building juggernaut of the London Borough of Lewisham but it drew attention to a transport policy that proposed to widen two major highways through Sydenham and Forest Hill. In 1943 the County of London Plan had proposed that a South Circular Road should be constructed as part of a co-ordinated road system. It would bypass Forest Hill by means of a tunnel. As a name, the South Circular Road could not be more inapt as it gives the impression that the road sweeps in a great

St Mary's Seminary,
Sydenham Hill.

Lammas Green estate, 2004.

arc across south London. Instead it meanders through narrow streets, many of which are main shopping streets, as is the case in Forest Hill. The 1943 proposal was abandoned but the problem of the South Circular remained. In 1989 it was proposed that a roundabout should be placed at the junction of London Road and Honor Oak Road and that a new road would cut behind Sainsbury's to link with Stanstead Road. Dartmouth Road would be closed from the traffic lights to Waldram Park Road and become a shopping area. A local MP, John Maples, led the objections to this. The one advantage seemed to be that buses and heavy traffic need not negotiate the left turn at Forest Hill traffic lights. The main disadvantages would be the extensive demolition of houses and the encouragement of more heavy traffic to use the South Circular. A South Circular Assessment Study, published by the Department of Transport, followed. The then Secretary of State, Cecil Parkinson, stated: 'I am only prepared to go forward with new road schemes which will bring significant overall benefits taking full account of the environmental effects'.

A new proposal to build tunnels at five places on the South Circular incorporated one at Forest Hill. Supplementary proposals, intended to placate objectors, included a new bus-rail interchange at Forest Hill and the potential for redevelopment in the area. The report did add disparagingly that 'the general area was not perceived to be attractive to business investment'. This did not placate the objectors, including the MPs in the Lewisham area. What killed the scheme, however, was the cost, estimated to exceed £870 million. Forest Hill was left to sort out its own traffic problems.

Halifax Street, 2004.

There were two proposals in the 1980s affecting traffic in Sydenham. Lewisham Council had closed Silverdale, a busy through route. A public enquiry led to this decision being reversed because so much traffic went through adjoining roads and the railway line blocked any new roads to the west. The second proposal affected a wider area. This was part of a scheme, known as HH4, to create an inner ring road round London and a major highway from Wandsworth through south London, along Southend Lane to join the A2 and the M20. A tunnel would go under Crystal Palace, Sydenham Road would be widened, shops demolished and side roads blocked. The Sydenham Society reported 'deep concern about the possibility of HH4 being chosen', surely an understatement. The projected 'corridor' for the new road was suggested to be up to half a mile wide. Rumours abounded that Sydenham Road would become a canyon and the total shopping area destroyed. The resulting uproar, together with the realisation of the overall cost, forced the government to abandon all proposals.

There have been improvements to public transport in south London. One was the extension of the Docklands Light Railway to Lewisham, although that did not directly benefit Sydenham and Forest Hill. Another has been the extension of the London Underground system. In 1902 it had been proposed to route an Underground line from Cannon Street through Wood Vale and under Sydenham Hill to Kirkdale. A later suggestion was to take the Bakerloo line from the Elephant and Castle through Forest Hill to Catford and Bromley. Both proposals sank into oblivion but what did survive was the possibility that Forest Hill and Sydenham could be linked to the London Underground. This has now been done. The East London Line now extends from Highbury and Islington to West Croydon with another line to Crystal Palace. There is a revival of interest in the areas and the line is well used, especially as an interchange at Canada Water allows commuters to reach Canary Wharf. It is also intended that Station Approach and parts of Sydenham Road will be improved to make it more amenable to pedestrians with the entrance to Queensthorpe Road blocked off and a small market area developed there.

One area that certainly is being changed is the former site of the South Eastern Gas Board in Bell Green. In 1969 after the gas board ceased production, Lewisham Borough Council saw this as ideal for retail development; but after considerable procrastination in 1999, the London Planning Advisory Committee decreed that it was unsuitable. Three years later, Sainsbury's proposal for a large retail store and petrol station was agreed. Inevitably many local shops closed. In 2003 British Gas submitted a planning application to develop the remainder of the site. A £19 million development, would include a Homebase superstore, a garden centre and other retail and industrial units to be the largest shopping centre in the area after Lewisham town centre, with a total retail area greater than that in Forest Hill. The Sydenham Society drew attention to the inevitable increase of traffic on already congested roads and the demise of local shops. Since then attitudes have changed. Shops and flats have been demolished at Bell Green, new flats are being built and some are being built close to Sainsbury's, although the large retail development seems to be in abeyance.

What does the future hold? Sydenham and Forest Hill were once part of an open landscape which seemed idyllic for those venturing forth from London. The railway and the coming of the Crystal Palace eventually turned what had been rural Kent into a built-up suburb of London. One of the last remaining parts of the Great North Wood has been preserved in the Sydenham Hill Woods nature reserve. The creation of the present townscape is perhaps due more to the London Borough of Lewisham than to the Luftwaffe in the Second World War. Local shops provide basic necessities and sometimes more exotic fare. Somewhat surprisingly, there is a constant rejuvenation: as one shop closes, another opens. It seems that both areas still thrive on local enterprise.

Sydenham and Forest Hill have tried to keep a village feel to their local centres and the creation of conservation areas has helped this. Crystal Palace Park and the local parks are well used. A mixed population includes older residents devoted to the area, newcomers drawn by the East London Line and a transient population that finds it a convenient commuting area. The 2010 census revealed that the population was mainly in its thirties and that there was a mixed ethnic population. Many languages can be heard in shops and in the street. Change is endemic in any society and this area of London seems continually to change. It may still be possible to agree with C. Edgar Thomas' words of a hundred years ago that the area has 'points of interest worthy of notice by the antiquary'.

Walking tours

Walk 1

Start at the corner of Sydenham Road and Trewsbury Road.

On Trewsbury Road is All Saints' church. The exterior belies an impressive interior. The architect George Fellowes Prynne was commissioned to provide a church seating at least 700 people 'in a free treatment of the fifteenth-century style'. This free treatment is notable in the screen dividing the chancel from the nave. The old chapel was converted into flats in 1999. Opposite, from 1920, was Criterion Ices, founded by the Valenti family, which closed to general regret in 2000; it still thrives at Thurston, Bury St Edmunds supplying ices to London. The building is now a restaurant.

Cross Sydenham Road and walk up it, passing the Dolphin and the Golden Lion.

The former Dissenters' chapel, now converted into housing.

After crossing the road, look down the other side. Next to the church hall is the eighteenth-century house called The Firs which, although somewhat dilapidated, is still impressive. Nos 122 and 124 were formerly one house; No. 120, now converted to a garage, was the manse for the Dissenters' chapel. Further down, a row of shops built in around 1900 is largely unaltered. On the corner of Kent House Road is the Prince Alfred, called after the second son of Queen Victoria, built as a beer house in around 1862, and now looking very smart after renovation.

Both the Golden Lion and the Dolphin pubs have a long history. The Golden Lion is first mentioned in 1747, when John Robinson 'of the Golden Lion' is recorded as being buried at St Mary's churchyard, Lewisham. Slightly damaged by bombing in 1944, the present building reflects solid Victorian architecture. Almost opposite, the Dolphin is first mentioned in 1733 in the parish register of St Mary's Lewisham, when Stephen, son of Richard Peake 'of Sipenham ye Dolphin', was buried in the churchyard. Like the Golden Lion, it survived the Second World War but had a chequered history in the 1990s when it was renamed the Ferret and Trouser Leg. Bus passengers who were accustomed to ask for the stop at the Dolphin were reluctant to use the new name. The original name has now been restored.

Further up, before crossing the road, look at the row of shops on the right, which still form a fine block. Grand Parade, as it was once known, was built in 1900 by the builders Edmundson & Sons and covered the front gardens of the Old House, owned by the Mayow Adams family. The new stretch between Nos 73 and 85 is a 1950s rebuild after a bomb jettisoned by a Junkers 88 blasted the shops in 1943. The Mayow Adams family had owned land almost to Perry Vale, some of which had already been sold for the canal and for Mayow Park. The family also created Mayow Road to open up the estate for development and provide a route between Sydenham and Forest Hill.

Turn right into Mayow Road and walk up the road, passing Earlsthorpe and Bishopsthorpe Roads; turn left into Mayow Park.

Mayow Park, originally called Sydenham Recreation Ground, opened in 1878 'for ever to be devoted to public use' after a campaign led by the Revd William Taylor Jones. A fountain in the park commemorates his work. 10,000 people were said to have attended the opening of the park. The ground for the bowling green and the tennis courts was raised in 1903. To the north are five blocks of flats, erected in 1962 on the Dacres estate.

Walk straight through the park, exit into Recreation Road and turn left into Silverdale.

Fountain commemorating William Taylor Jones.

The north side of Recreation Road has altered little since the houses were built in the 1880s, although No. 9 was one of the few houses to be damaged by bombs in the Second World War. To the right, along Silverdale, which becomes Dacres Road, is the Dietrich Bonhoeffer church. Silverdale was badly bombed during the Second World War and many Victorian houses were destroyed. Others were demolished by Lewisham Council to build blocks of flats of the type which Pevsner has described as 'plentiful but unmemorable' so that pre-war Silverdale is now unrecognisable.

Turn left into Bishopsthorpe Road, right into Queensthorpe Road, then right again into Sydenham Road.

The Thorpe estate, or The Thorpes as it is now known, is on the grounds of the Old House. The names of the roads all bear a noble first part: Kings-, Queens-, Princes-, Dukes-, Earls- and Bishops-. Building began at Bishopsthorpe Road in around 1904 and ended with Dukesthorpe Road in the 1920s. Most of the

Lewisham Borough Council flats in Silverdale.

Bishopsthorpe Road, c. 1909.

houses retain their original features and were incorporated into a conservation area in 2002.

Both Bishopsthorpe and Queensthorpe Roads are almost the same as when they were built in the early twentieth century. One addition is Cobbsthorpe Villas, built on the site of a garage, which in turn had replaced Salter's nursery gardens. Opposite Queensthorpe Road is the nondescript Narborhood Centre built on the site of the Queen's Hall cinema. Further up are Woodman's Cottage and Priory Cottage, a handsome semi-detached pair of cottages, almost Dutch in appearance with hipped roofs and rendered fronts. These were probably built in the early eighteenth century as timber buildings, as can still be seen at the side, with a brick front added later. They are possibly the oldest surviving houses in Sydenham; their appearance in this busy high street is a complete surprise.

Continue up Sydenham Road, crossing over the railway bridge.

Sydenham station originally had two entrances, as the platforms were not opposite to each other. The entrance for the up platform on the opposite side of the road closed in 1982. The first station was built in 1839 on the bed of the former Croydon Canal; the present station opened in 1875. Sydenham is now part of the busy East London Line with connections to Canary Wharf and the East End.

The Railway public house dates back to 1868 but was partly rebuilt after bomb damage in the Second World War. The Greyhound, now undergoing complete refurbishment and with blocks of flats on its one spacious car park, has the distinction of being Sydenham's oldest public house although the front part is an addition of 1873. First mentioned in 1727, it provided refreshment, and bed and board, for those visiting the Wells, and profitably served both the navvies who dug the canal and those who created the railway. These were tough men. In 1837, just before the railway opened, there was an altercation at the Greyhound between the landlord, William Ridgeway, and a railway worker, James Hockham. Ridgeway had refused to serve Hockham, who retaliated. Ridgeway called the constables, whereupon the navvies turned on the landlord. When Hockham was brought before the magistrates he was fined £5 but another navvy named Brown, who had supported him, was fined only 10s. The difference was that Coulson, the railway superintendent, had sent the magistrates a letter supporting Brown.

The junction of Sydenham Road, Westwood Hill and Kirkdale is still dominated by Cobbs Corner. Walter Cobb opened a small shop here in 1860, later adding more shops to build a corner extension with a distinctive dome in 1902. He even extended across the road into Nos 270 and 272 Kirkdale. The department store flourished and, in spite of being badly bombed in 1940, continued until the 1970s. Even today, with the building turned into small shops and a fitness club and disfigured on the façade by air-conditioning units, it still retains some of its former grandeur. The former Old Cedars, now the Excelcare Kirkdale Care Centre, at the bottom of Westwood Hill is impressive probably because of the large expanse of ground in front of it. The middle part is the original house dating from the 1780s and its eighteenth-century appearance can be more clearly seen from the back; to the left is an extension dating from 1870 and to the right an extension built in the 1990s.

Continue up Westwood Hill

On the corner with Lawrie Park Road is an Italianate villa dating from the 1860s. Almost opposite is St Bartholomew's church, built by Lewis Vulliamy in 1832. Later Edwin Nash added the apsidal chancel and the north aisle, which has been widened to become a vestry. The height of the interior is impressive, as are the modern stained-glass windows in the chancel; the east window depicts Christ in Glory. The handsome clock tower with its castellated top features in Pissarro's painting of 'The Avenue at Sydenham'. By the path is the grave of the twelve workmen who were killed in 1853 when they fell while building the

The Greyhound, c. 1904.

The Greyhound, 2004.

Cobbs Corner.

Crystal Palace. The adjoining tabletop tomb surrounded by iron railings is the tomb of Robert and Elizabeth Harrild who owned Round Hill House.

Beyond the church is St David's, where the Antarctic explorer Sir Ernest Shackleton lived. The Victorian houses between here and Jew's Walk show traces of Strawberry Hill Gothic design. They were neglected in the 1960s and inhabited by squatters but have been rescued. Several have been turned into flats. Nos 18 and 20 have strange dragonesque carved heads, which act as gargoyles above the windows. No. 24 has been more carefully restored with a Welsh slate roof and the original style of windows.

Turn right into Jew's Walk.

There has been speculation about this name but it is generally agreed that it came from David Ximenes, who planted the road with elms. It was replanted with chestnut trees in the 1850s. David Ximenes was son of Sir Moses Ximenes, scion of an old Spanish Jewish family that had fled from the Inquisition. Like Disraeli's father, Sir Moses disagreed with the committee of Bevis Marks synagogue and converted to Christianity. Like Disraeli, David Ximenes was still regarded as Jewish by the public, hence the road's name. He bought Westwood House in 1766 and the family lived there for a few years. From 1899 it was the Passmore Edwards orphanage. After the Second World War the site was sold for the Shenewood estate. Jew's Walk still contains some fine houses of the 1850s, again mainly displaying Tudor and Gothic features and some handsome porches. The house on the corner has gargoyle heads. No. 13 is of red brick with white facings. Two houses are of red brick with grey brick patterning. At No. 7 Jew's Walk lived Karl Marx's daughter, Eleanor, who committed suicide here in 1898. The doctor who was called to her was Ernest Shackleton's father, Henry.

Turn left into Longton Grove, then right into Longton Avenue.

These wide roads were part of the estate developed by Major Forster on land he had secured as part of the enclosure of Westwood Common. In spite of extensive bomb damage, many fine houses still remain which reflect the solid comfort expected by their inhabitants when they bought them in the 1850s. Nos 6-12 show the extent of the bombing: Nos 6 and 12 retain their classical grandeur while where Nos 8-10 once stood is filled by a plain block. The original houses were of classical style. They utilised grey London bricks enhanced by white stone dressings, and had square porches. Many of the houses are now divided into flats.

Longton Avenue shows the post-war building of Lewisham Borough Council. Large blocks of flats have been built on the left side. The right side still keeps its classical charm. No. 6 Longton Avenue is a sturdily built symmetrical building; Nos 8 and 10 have apsed rooms on the ground and first floors. No. 17 Longton Avenue and the adjoining houses in Ormanton Road are of a different variety, being based on Walter Segal's self-build concept. Segal was a Swiss architect

St Bartholomew's church tower.

Dragonesque carved heads, Westwood Hill.

Walter Segal's self-build concept housing, Ormanton Road.

who came to London in the 1950s believing that people could and should be able to build their own homes. Lewisham Council supported his ideas but few houses were built. These timber structures, built in 1982, provide evidence of his ideas put into practice. They are somewhat Swiss in appearance with their chalet-style roofs.

Opposite the end of Ormanton Road is an entrance to Sydenham Wells Park. Go into the park and down the path to the large pond.

The eighteen-acre park is larger than it seems because flats truncate the view. The name comes from the Wells that made Sydenham famous in the eighteenth century. A park was necessary for the working people in this area because Mayow Park was a mile away and Crystal Palace Park was not free. Revd A.E. King, vicar of St Philip's, fought to save land from development so part of the former Westwood Common was turned into a park by London County Council after 1898, and formally opened in 1901, with a bandstand, tennis courts and a quoits pitch. The tennis courts survive and a putting green and a dry football pitch have been added.

At the large pond, go to the left, noting two more ponds fed by freshwater streams. Return to the larger pond, now the haunt of several species of water birds. Bear to the right of the main pond and follow the path running by the side of Taylor's Lane.

An exit leads into the lane, and it is well-worth going into the lane to see the few remaining cottages, which still give the lane a rural charm; note especially Nos 12-14 and Nos 59-61. Two other cottages have kept the weatherboarding in the upper storey. The Wells Park estate has replaced almost all the rest.

Return to the park, pass the children's play area, which was originally the paddling pool, and exit by the next gate into Taylor's Lane. Turn left, then right into Wells Park Road.

On the corner once stood St Philip's church, built in 1865 by Edwin Nash and reputed to be on the site of the most important Well. Badly damaged during wartime, it was demolished in 1982, to be replaced by a low building. In the garden is a bell from the old church. The schoolroom, also by Nash, survives and is used by the Seventh Day Adventists. Little of Wells Road, now Wells Park Road, survives in its original form. It was bombed in 1943 and 1944 and, rather than repair the old cottages, Lewisham Council decided to demolish streets such as Bradford Road and replace them with blocks of flats in the 1960s and 1970s. Some of the cottages had origins going back to the Wells, the most famous one being Mill Cottage, often called the Green Dragon, which was demolished by a flying bomb in 1944.

The Talma which predates the demolition era was built in the 1880s, replacing a building of 1863. The name is said to come from a French actor, Jean Talma (1763-1826), and the pub sign shows him in a classical role. For a time a music hall provided the patrons with additional entertainment. Diagonally opposite, Nos 104 replaces The Duke first named the Duke of Edinburgh, after the second son of Queen Victoria, and later after the actor, John Wayne. The line of shops marks the site of the Beehive pub, which closed in 1866.

Further down, Mill Gardens marks the site of the mill erected in around 1837 by William Atherfold and run by the Brigden family from the 1840s to the 1880s. The mill was pulled down in the 1880s but the buildings survived until the whole area was cleared. It is a surprise to find that Halifax Street has survived as a curved street running round to join Kirkdale. This gives an idea of what the area was like before the 1960s. Neat semi-detached and terraced cottages and an Italianate terrace retain their Victorian charm.

Wells Park, now Wells Park Road, c. 1910.

Wells Cottage, the former Green Dragon, was rebuilt in around 1900 and was probably the oldest building in Sydenham. It was destroyed by bombing in 1944.

At the end of Wells Park Road, turn left into Kirkdale.

This makes a good viewpoint. At the end of the road is Farnboro House, a stucco-rendered villa dating from around 1840 with a large apsed room to the right and a fine porch with Tuscan columns. At the end of Jew's Walk is an ornate fountain with ornate baroque-type volutes, commemorating the Jubilee of Queen Victoria and restored by the Sydenham Society for the Silver Jubilee of the present Queen. Behind it, retirement flats stand on the site of a preparatory school attended by Sir Ernest Shackleton. In Jew's Walk is Grove House, its neat porch supported by Ionic pillars. This is the centre for the adjoining Grove Centre church, a Baptist and United Reformed church which replaced the Congregational church built in 1867 and demolished in 1973.

Across the road is the Church of the Resurrection with a striking statue of the risen Christ on its façade. The church replaces the former St Bartholomew's National School. Sydenham Park, which runs by the side of the church, is one of several roads laid out on the site of the canal reservoir.

Fox's, previously The Fox and Hounds and the Woodman public houses recall that Westwood Common originally extended across this area. The terrace dates from around 1900. This part of Kirkdale was originally known as Sydenham High Street and served as a shopping centre for Sydenham before it moved to Sydenham Road. A drinking fountain for horses stood at the junction of the roads.

Continue up Kirkdale, known until 1936 as Sydenham Hill Road.

On the corner, two timber-boarded houses survive from the 1820s and give a taste of how much of Sydenham may have looked at that period. Opposite is the Kirkdale Learning Centre. This was originally the Sydenham Lecture Hall built in 1861 to a design by Joseph Paxton, hence the still handsome front with

Farnboro House, c. 1840.

Sydenham High Street, c. 1915. A horse trough stood at the road junction. To the right, beyond the tall buildings, can be seen two timber-boarded houses dating from around 1820.

The Green Man carved on the capital of a house on the corner of Mount Gardens.

Renaissance features. Behind is Kelvin Grove School, a typical London School Board building built in 1873, with a smaller building added by London County Council in 1902. Although Kelvin Grove was bombed in the war, some handsome Italianate buildings of the 1860s survive.

Further up is Panmure Road, which suffered severely when it was hit by a V2 in January 1945; at least ten houses and St Matthew's church were destroyed. Then comes Mount Ash Road with similar terraced houses lining either side of the street. These have changed little since they were built in the 1870s, although they are probably in better condition now than when they were first built with the intention of being sold to middle-class Victorian commuters.

Beyond this is Mount Gardens, a narrow lane that divides into two and still retains a rural aspect. Along a narrow road to the right are Ash Tree Cottage and the former Roussell Cottage, two excellently preserved weatherboarded cottages, now knocked into one, slightly earlier in date than those in Kirkdale. Further up, Hazeldine Cottage was originally provided for servants who worked at a large house on Sydenham Hill. Note the Victorian letterbox inset in the porch, inserted by the previous owners. The other lane leads to two more cottages of the 1820s: Oak House built in the early 1900s and The Orchard which dates from around 1820.

Continue up Kirkdale until its junction with Sydenham Hill.

At the junction is Eliot Bank, still an unadopted road, which takes its name from the family name of the Earl of St Germans. Oak Cottage on the left has twin gables and these are reflected in details on the terrace of Julian Taylor Path directly opposite. Phoenix House, a mixture of the Tudor and Gothic styles which are such a feature of buildings in Sydenham, was built in the 1850s.

From here the path drops towards London Road, opposite the Horniman Museum, where it is possible to join Walk 2. Otherwise, before returning down Kirkdale, stand at the junction of Kirkdale and Sydenham Hill and sample the impressive view to the north-west of the Dawson Heights flats and the City of London's towers.

right Hazeldine Cottage before restoration.

far right Hazeldine Cottage, 2004.

Walk 2

Dartmouth Road leads towards Forest Hill. In the nineteenth century, the southern part of the road was part of the Sydenham High Street, with small shops and several beer houses. It now contains few shops, owing to the destruction caused in 1941 when a land mine exploded killing at least twenty-one people. The corner where the restored 1924 Bricklayer's Arms with its punning inn sign is situated was one of the few surviving parts. Willow Way is a reminder of the willows lining the Croydon Canal reservoir, which occupied this area to top up the waters of the canal.

Opposite is Sydenham School. The main building is a 1917 imposing red brick building with a Classical façade. When comprehensive education began, the site was expanded. In 1957 Sir Basil Spence, the foremost architect of the day, built a modern block. This was delicately supported on piers so that the ground floor was left open, but to create more interior space the openings were enclosed in 1994. In 1973 a library and Sixth Form centre were added, thus breaking the original design.

Beyond the school, turn up Round Hill.

A curiosity is the upper part of the steeple of St Antholin, once situated in Watling Street in the City of London and built by Sir Christopher Wren, probably in around 1678. The church was demolished in 1875 and the spire was bought by Robert Harrild, and placed at Round Hill House as an interesting folly. Lewisham Borough Council bought Round Hill House, an acre of land and the spire for £18,250 and incorporated the spire into a housing estate. At the end of Round Hill turn right to reach Baxter Field, named after George Baxter who, in the 1830s, was the first to make cheap colour printing possible, thereby providing affordable pictures. The open space commemorates him.

Sydenham School building dating from 1917.

Return to Dartmouth Road, cross the road and walk down Sydenham Park Road.

Steeple of St Antholin, Round Hill.

Sydenham Park was part of the Sydenham Park estate developed after 1842, mainly by Robert Harrild of Round Hill House. This area was popular with city clerks, especially as it was within walking distance of Forest Hill station. Albion Villas Road ends in what appears to be rural setting, which was the site of the Upper Sydenham Lawn Tennis Club until 1985. When it closed, a proposal to erect thirty-five houses was successfully opposed. It is now the Millennium Green site, designated as being of ecological importance, and is one of the few remaining areas of Westwood Common. Both Albion Villas Road and Redberry Grove contain interesting houses, as does Sydenham Park Road. Holy Trinity church, near the corner of Sydenham Park Road, was demolished in 1981 to be replaced by Trinity Court. Turning left along Sydenham Park Road leads to a footbridge crossing the railway, giving access to Dacres Road by the Dietrich Bonhoeffer church. Turning right leads along Sydenham Park with yet more examples of handsome houses, most now turned into flats.

Return to Dartmouth Road and turn right.

George Baxter.

The roads to the right are former slipways leading to what were the former canal wharves. Go down one of these to follow the line of the towpath to Forest Hill station. Alexander Hennell, a devotee of the Arts and Crafts movement, designed Forest Hill Library, recently completely refurbished. There is an impressive cupola, a terracotta frieze with delightful putti, and a striking Venetian window. The interior is light and airy with no feeling of repressive scholarship. Next comes Louise House, built in 1890 by Thomas Aldwinckle, which is built of red brick with a Gothic doorway and a terracotta-tiled frieze. Then follows Forest Hill Swimming Pools, built in red brick by the same architect in 1885. These, reputed to be the oldest baths in London, have been saved from closure and are being rebuilt to provide two modern pools, a gymnasium and rooms for community use.

Castellated doorway, Sydenham Park Road.

Behind No. 31 was a boathouse which hired out boats on the canal. The Dartmouth Arms once served the bargees of the Croydon Canal and also provided a tea garden for more genteel patrons. The pub was rebuilt in 1866. On the corner of Dartmouth Road and London Road is Barclays bank, enhanced by the oriel window on the first floor.

The original Dartmouth Arms station, built in 1839, was in the space between W.H. Smith's and the present station. This was renamed Forest Hill six years later. The next station in 1854 was placed to the south of W.H. Smith's. It in turn was rebuilt in 1883 as a grandiose building with an impressive tower, which was badly damaged when the subway received a direct hit from a V2 in June 1944. It was rebuilt in its present utilitarian style in the 1970s. The subway by the side leads to Perry Vale. Before turning left into London Road, go along Devonshire Road. The raised pavement on David's Road, where Nos 13-34 are prominent, marks the east towpath of the canal. Below is a mural created by James Salisbury.

Forest Hill Library, c. 1920.

Turn left along London Road

The Capitol public house was built as an art deco cinema in 1929. It later became a bingo hall and then closed in 1996. Destruction was averted by a J.D. Wetherspoon takeover, which has kept the impressive interior. The exterior still retains its decorative patterns, winged cherubs and lion heads. Further along London Road is the Dorrell estate. This, designed by Arthur Dorrell, was developed as long blocks in the Classical style. The square bays with Doric columns on the first floor were once entrances gained by impressive staircases. Nos 66-77 consist of two blocks built in 1840 and a detached villa, but are spoilt by an infill building dating from 1900. Another impressive 1840 block lies beyond, with further additions built in the early 1900s. In 1975 Lewisham Council bought the blocks and made further additions at the side and the rear.

At the top of the rise is the Horniman Museum and Gardens, both great favourites with teachers, parents and children. The gardens were originally the grounds of Surrey Mount, Frederick Horniman's home, and of other London Road houses. They provide a restful setting at any time of the year. Behind the museum is the exquisite conservatory which dates from 1894; it was designed for Horniman for his home at Coombe Cliffe, Croydon but moved to Forest Hill in 1988. This delicate structure is used for musical entertainments and as a café. By the side of the conservatory is one of several sundials in the gardens; it is a double polar sundial with the inscription: 'and hours run mad, e'en as men might', which seems peculiar until one realises that it is a somewhat loose anagram of The Horniman Museum and Gardens.

From the conservatory, the path to the left leads to the sunken garden. The main path leads to the bandstand and the Dutch barn, brought from Holland by Frederick Horniman. From here there is a magnificent view of the City of London, revealing St Paul's Cathedral, the former Natwest Tower, the bullet-shaped Swiss Re bank building and the arch of Wembley Stadium. The nearby ziggurat block is Dawson Heights, built between 1966 and 1972. To the right a

The Horniman Museum conservatory.

A rare survival. Telephone kiosks designed by Sir Giles Gilbert Scott outside the Capitol, Forest Hill. A K2 kiosk from 1924 is on the right and a K6 from 1935 on the left.

path leads to the exit into Horniman Drive; on the grass is another sundial. If you stand on the appropriate month of the analemmatic sundial, designed in 1994, your shadow will fall on the numbered slab giving the correct British Summer Time. In 2009, the museum was awarded Heritage Lottery Money for an extensive refurbishment of the gardens, which will be completed in 2012.

There is now a choice of routes. The main path continues round the gardens passing a concrete sports oval, the former toy boating pool. Beyond this, a way leads out of the gardens to the Horniman Nature Trail, which for some distance goes along the disused raised railway track of the Crystal Palace High Level Railway. The second route leads from the gardens into Westwood Park. Turn right and at the crossroads at the top there is a splendid view across south London. The green expanse of treetops makes it seem as like open countryside.

Turn left along Horniman Drive, turn left into Ringmore Rise and follow the road round. Bear right into Liphook Crescent and follow the Crescent to rejoin Horniman Drive.

Horniman Primary School, constructed in 1972, was built in tiers down the hill. It now has some handsome gates to its left. On the corner of Ringmore Rise is a 1934 house built by a maker of handbags and umbrellas, who became an amateur architect. The house was constructed in the style of an ocean liner. Through the gardens of Ringmore Rise are extensive views over London including the London Eye, St Paul's Cathedral, Tate Modern and as far west as Battersea Power Station. In Liphook Crescent, between No. 23 and its neighbour, can be seen an octagonal folly tower, previously a garden building of Tewkesbury Lodge (now demolished). Continue along Horniman Drive to enter the Horniman Gardens, where refreshments can be obtained in the museum café.

Telling the time at the analemmatic sundial in Horniman Gardens.

Walk 3

This walk takes in the Crystal Palace area and gives some idea of the extent of the area formerly laid out to Paxton's instructions.

Start on Crystal Palace Parade on the corner of Farquhar Road.

The view looks down on the former site of the High Level station, now utilised for housing. The last train ran in 1954 and the station was demolished in 1961. On the other side of Farquhar Road, the parking area marks the site of the turntable where engines were turned round. From this part of the parade, before 1936, it was possible to look along the length of the Crystal Palace frontage, which would have stretched as far as the site of the BBC television mast erected in 1954. To see the retaining wall with the original arcading, go down Farquhar Road and turn into Spinney Gardens. A stretch of wall leads to Paxton's tunnel, now closed, which emerged into what is now the Hillcrest estate.

Return to Crystal Palace Parade and cross the road, entering the park by the corner gate.

Note two handsome metal direction signs before the gate. Take the path through the flowerbeds. To the left is a grassed area with a headless nymph, one of the few statues left in the park because those that had survived were almost all sold by London County Council in 1957, to prevent them being vandalised. The nymph marks the spot where Osler's Crystal Fountain once stood, the meeting place for Palace visitors. On this site a beacon is erected and lighted to mark significant events such as the 400th anniversary of the defeat of the Spanish Armada in 1988, the Silver Jubilee in 1977 and the Golden Jubilee in 2002.

The retaining wall of the former High Level station.

Direction sign to Crystal Palace Parade.

Go down the steps with iron railings.

To the right is the base of the South Tower, built by Isambard Kingdom Brunel in 1856 as one of a pair to contain the water for the fountains. In 1940 it was dismantled, in stages rather than by a controlled fall as happened to the North Tower. By its side is a small museum, which is open at the weekends and bank holidays from 11 a.m.–3 p.m. in Winter, 11 a.m–4.30 p.m. in Summer, with photographs, films and exhibits giving the story of the Palace. The building originally housed a School of Practical Engineering, run by the Crystal Palace Company.

Go ahead from the museum and follow the path ahead.

This brings you to a bank from which it is possible to survey the length of the Lower Terrace, which is 1,640ft (500m) long. The grassy area was the first of the garden terraces, once laid out as a formal Italian garden with flowerbeds, fountains and statuary, among which an admiring throng of people walked. Only the retaining walls and the bases marking the central avenue survive. This area was used for the magnificent weekly firework displays prepared by Brock and usually ending with a fiery tableau.

Go down the steps between the sphinxes and walk along the Upper Terrace.

Shell brick copy of sphinx at Taris. One of the remaining guardians of the terrace steps.

From here there are splendid views across south London and Kent. The masts over the athletics track are clearly visible and the slanted roof to the right is the site of the Low Level station, from which visitors entered the park by a covered way. The balustrade is still in place and two statues remain. The bearded, turbaned one is the last of a group representing inhabitants of the once vast British Empire. The sphinxes guarding the steps are shell brick copies of a sphinx found at Tanis. At the end of the terrace are more sphinxes and the wall of the orangery. During the hurricane of October 1987, 400 trees in the grounds were blown down and a further 1,000 damaged. A policy of replanting has made good some of the losses.

Continue along the Upper Terrace then descend to the Lower Terrace. Go left to follow the base of the terrace. Bear diagonally right to re-enter the park grounds and follow the path sloping down.

To the left is the former Concert Bowl. During the 1980s and 1990s concerts were regularly given during the summer, often ending with a firework display, visible over the Sydenham area. Continue past the Bowl to reach the restored Maze. When it was laid out in 1870, it was one of the biggest in the world: 160ft (49m) in diameter, constructed of hornbeam hedges. It was termed the Tea Maze because it was considered fashionable for ladies to walk in it at around four o'clock in the afternoon. In the Second World War it was allowed to grow wild, but has now been restored to mark the centenary of Girlguiding

UK. During a Boy Scout rally in the park in 1909 a group of girls approached Robert Baden-Powell to demand a similar organization and the guiding movement was founded. Turn right to follow the retaining terrace wall. From here, it is possible to admire the quality of the stone and the strength of the wall. A headless statue of Dante is below the wall. Re-enter the palace area. Continue to the terrace steps and turn left. Before the sports area is the head of Paxton by W.F. Woodington, better known for his sculpture of the Coade stone lion on Westminster Bridge.

The National Sports Centre is on the site of the Great Fountain basins. The sports hall and the baths were completed in 1964 and the athletics stadium in 1977. At that time they were among the finest facilities in Britain and are listed as Grade II. They are in need of updating but are still used as a sports venue. It is hoped to up date the facilities in time for the Olympics in 2012. Beyond the hall is the model-car racing track. The park was used for motor racing from 1923 until the fire and again from 1953 to 1973, when a new track was created.

Go between the hall and the stadium, descend all the steps and go to the left.

A wooden shelter is surrounded by flowerbeds. During the First World War, the Palace became HMS *Victory VI*, a Royal Naval Volunteer Reserve training establishment of up to 125,000 men. The bell, which once stood on the Lower Terrace, then regarded as the quarterdeck, was placed here in 1931. The open space and the children's play area was originally the site of the London County Cricket Club ground on which W.G. Grace played. Until 1909 he lived at No. 7 Lawrie Park Road, a convenient residence for attending the matches.

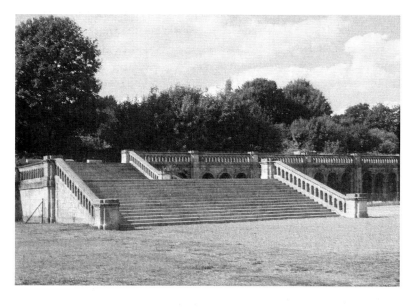

The terrace steps, 2003.

The bell of HMS *Crystal Palace*.

Retrace your steps, go past the Grand Central Walk, enter the enclosure containing the boating lake and dinosaurs and bear left, then right towards the Irish Elks.

The directors of the Crystal Palace Company aimed to attract, entertain and educate. The dinosaur area, begun in 1852, did all three, with the intention of providing a journey through 350 million years of prehistoric time from the Ice Age to the Triassic period, beginning with the Irish Elks and ending with the Dicynodonts. Benjamin Waterhouse Hawkins built thirty-three of these monsters under the direction of Sir Richard Owen, superintendent of the Natural History Museum. Hawkins, who was given the title of Director of the Fossil Department of the Crystal Palace, constructed them according to the knowledge of the day. Since then, far more has been discovered about these prehistoric beasts and today many would be a very different shape. Bromley Council, together with the Heritage Lottery Fund and the Single Regeneration Fund, have raised £4 million to restore this area of the park to its original design and the dinosaurs to how they looked when first constructed. They are still a popular attraction, but unfortunately there are no plans to restore the boating lake to its full glory.

The dinosaur trail begins with the Irish Elk or Megaloceros, the male standing proudly displaying its huge antlers. Bear left to pass Megatherium, the giant sloth – Hawkins managed to reproduce its shaggy hair – and follow the path round to see Mosasaurus, a gigantic lizard, lurking in the water. Behind the lizard, the first of the Pterodactyls flaps giant wings. On the bank are a family of Anoplotherium and Palaeotherium, the latter having short trunked features. These were probably the ancestors of modern elephants. Cross the stone bridge, bear left and cross a second bridge. On the right is the Time Trail, which was part of the educational mission of the directors. Here are limestone cliffs, and coal and ironstone seams.

To the left is the first dinosaur island. On this can be found Iguanodons, Pterodactyls, the spiked Hylaeosaurus and a hunchbacked Megalosaurus, which is now known to have walked on its hind legs. In the water are Teleosaurus, with its long snout and fearsome teeth, and long-necked Plesiosaurs. At the end of this island group are Ichthyosaurs, said to be an ancestor of modern dolphins, and Labyrinthodonts, ancestors of modern newts, but Owen's interpretation of them made them look like frogs. Round the end are Dicynodonts looking something like turtles, with a wrongly attributed shellback. The restoration aims to place each of these monsters in the setting of rocks and vegetation that would have been its habitat, so in that way the directors' view of educating the people could be said to continue.

Either walk around the boating lake or return to the Irish Elks and exit the enclosure by the park café.

The Giant Sloth.

The café is always popular and there is an information centre, which has changing exhibitions relating to the renewal of the park. From here can be seen the Grand Central Walk. It was originally 2,600ft (793m) long and 96ft (29m) wide and led towards the Palace building but now only reaches the sports area. Here it is possible to leave the park by the Penge Gate.

Further reading

Sydenham has had three local newspapers, all of which have ceased publication. These were the *Forest Hill, Penge and Sydenham Examiner* (1895-1933), the *Sydenham, Forest Hill and Penge Gazette* (1873-1974) and the *Sydenham Times* (1861-1883). Since their demise, the area has been served by the *Kentish Mercury* (1839-present). The Lewisham History Society has a newsletter and has published several articles on Sydenham in the *Lewisham Local History Society Transactions* (1963-1988) and the *Lewisham History Journal* (1993-2003). The Sydenham Society, founded in 1972, produces the *Sydenham Society News* four times a year and this often has reminiscences by local residents and information on the area. The Kirkdale Bookshop holds occasional exhibitions of the work of local artists and old photographs of the area.

Adams, J., *A History of Kings and Princes Garth and Forest Hill*, 1993.

Adams, M.W., *Sydenham*, 1878.

Beattie, W., *Life and Letters of Thomas Campbell*, 1850.

Beaver, P., *The Crystal Palace 1851-1936: A Portrait of Victorian Enterprise*, 1970.

Besant, W., *London South of the Thames*, 1912.

Bird, A., *Paxton's Palace*, 1976.

Blake, L., *Bolts from the Blue: SE London and Kent under V2 Rocket Attack*, 1990.

Blake, L., *Red Alert: South East London 1939-1945*, 1992.

Booth, C., *Life and Labour of the People of London, Volume VI: Religious Influences, Outer South East London*, 1902.

Cherry, B. and Pevsner, N., *The Buildings of England. London 2: South*, 1982.

Colquhoun, K., *A Thing in Disguise: The Visionary Life of Joseph Paxton*, 2003.

Coulter, J., *Lewisham History and Guide*, 1994.

Coulter, J. and Seaman, J., *Archive Photographs Series: Sydenham and Forest Hill*, 1995.

Coulter, J. and Seaman, J., *Forest Hill and Sydenham*. Britain in Old Photographs, 2003.

Coulter, J., *Sydenham and Forest Hill Past*, 1999.

Duncan, L.L., *History of the Borough of Lewisham*, 1908.

George, K., *Two Sixpences Please: Lewisham's Early Cinemas*, 1986.

George, K., *The Big Five: Lewisham's Super Cinemas*, 1997.

Hadfield, C., *The Canals of South and South-East England*, 1969.

Hadfield, C., *Atmospheric Railways*, 1967.

Hasted, E., *The History and Topographical Survey of the County of Kent, 1795*, (ed. Everitt, A.), 1972.

Hollis, B.R., *The Forgotten Front Line: Station 40 New Cross*, 1985.

Holt, J., *My Early Years in Sydenham*, 2007

Hook, J., *The Air Raids on London during the 1914-1918 War, Booklet No. 12: The Raids on Lewisham*, 1989.

Hook, J., *They Shall Not Grow Old: Air Raids on Lewisham 1940-45*, 1995.

Howard-Turner, J.T., *The London, Brighton and South Coast Railway* (3 volumes), 1977-79.

Hutchings, W.W., *London Town, Past and Present* (2 volumes), 1909.

Imperial War Graves Commission, *War Dead 1939-1945: Metropolitan Borough of Lewisham*, 1954.

Johnson, D.R., *Around Crystal Palace and Penge*, 2004.

Leith, I., *Delamotte's Crystal Palace*, 2005.

Margary, I., *Roman Roads in Britain*, 1968.

Markham, V.R., *Paxton and the Bachelor Duke*, 1935.

Marshall, D., *A History of the Southern Railway, Volume I*, 1946.

McKean, J., *Crystal Palace, Joseph Paxton and Charles Fox*, 1994.

McKeown, A., *A Beacon of Hope: A History of a Sydenham Parish (The Parish of Our Lady and St Philip Neri)*, 2001.

Mudie-Smith, R., *The Religious Life of London*, 1906.

Nisbet, J., *The Story of One Tree Hill Agitation*, 1997.

Piggott, J.P., *Palace of the People: The Crystal Palace at Sydenham*, 2004.

Prockter, A., *Forest Hill and Sydenham*, 1987.

Prockter, A., *The London and Croydon Railway*, 1989.

Pullen, D., *Sydenham*, 1975.

Pullen, D., *Forest Hill*, 1979.

Ramsey, W. (ed.), *The Blitz: Then and Now* (3 volumes), 1987-90.

Reed, N., *Camille Pissarro at Crystal Palace*, 1987.

Reed, N., *Crystal Palace and the Norwoods*, 1995.

Rees, A., *Cyclopaedia*, 1819.

Routledge's *Guide to the Crystal Palace and Park at Sydenham*, 1854.

Salter, B., *Retracing Canals to Croydon and Camberwell*, 1986.

Snowden, C., *Tudor Hall: The First Hundred Years, 1850-1946*.

Spurgeon, D., *Discover Sydenham and Catford*, 1999.

Thorne, J., *Handbook to the Environs of London*, 1876.

Timpson's *Church History of Kent*, 1859.

Trotter, W.E., *The Croydon Railway and its Adjoining Survey*, 1838.

Walford, E., *London South of the Thames*, 1895.

Walker, P., *Welcome to our Church: Dietrich Bonhoeffer Church, Sydenham*, 1999.

Walker, P., 'The Story of the German Church in Sydenham', *Lewisham History Journal*, 11, 2003, pp. 1–32.

Wallenberg, J.K., *Kentish Place Names*, 1931.

Warwick, A.R., *The Phoenix Suburb: A South London Social History*, 1973.

Waterhouse-Hopkins, B., *Guide to the Crystal Palace and the Park*, 1877.

White, K., *The Public Houses of Lee and Lewisham*, 1992.

Yardley, M.D. (ed.), *Sydenham High School 1887-1987: Century Reminiscences*, 1987.

Index